SCIENCE
ALL AROUND

by
ROBIN KERROD

PURNELL

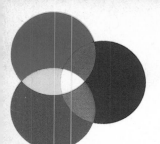

Contents

Published by Purnell Books
Berkshire House, Queen Street, Maidenhead
SBN 361 04406 2
Designed and produced by Grisewood & Dempsey Ltd
Grosvenor House, 141/143 Drury Lane, London WC2B 5TG
© Grisewood & Dempsey Ltd 1979
Printed and bound by Vallardi Industrie Grafiche, Milan

How, When and Where

ONCE upon a time people believed in fairy stories and wonders – in seven-league boots, in witches flying on broomsticks, in mirrors that talked, machines that could fly to the moon, in fact, in all manner of marvels. Today we live in an age of real marvels. By telephone we can speak to friends in every corner of the earth; by airliner we can be whisked, as on a magic carpet, to far off places; with computers we can, in a twinkling of an electronic eye, calculate the most complex of mathematical riddles; and perhaps, most amazing of all, by spacecraft we can travel to the moon and penetrate the depths of space.

Such modern marvels have resulted from centuries of science. The word science means knowledge, and particularly, knowledge gained by observation and experiment. Scientists not only observe what happens in the world about us, they try to find out how and why it happens. They investigate the nature and properties of

A toy gyroscope can balance on the point of a pencil – once its wheel has been set spinning. As the wheel slows down, the gyroscope loses its balance and eventually topples over. Bicycles and motorbikes work on exactly the same principle: their wheels are gyroscopes.

A flash of lightning (left) is a gigantic spark of electricity which jumps from one cloud to another or from a cloud to the ground. The lightning heats the air it passes through. Thunder is the sound of the heated air rapidly expanding.

Sunlight is a mixture of all the colours of the rainbow. An object appears to have a certain colour because it reflects light of that colour into our eyes. A red object absorbs all the colours of light except red. It reflects red light into our eyes and therefore appears to be red. Nature's dramatic colours are all created in this way.

When air is heated it expands and becomes lighter. In a hot-air balloon (right), air is heated by a jet of burning gas. The balloon rises when the weight of the heated gas plus the balloon and its passengers is lighter than the surrounding air.

The force of heated, expanding steam is used to power a steam engine. The picture (left) shows how great the force of expansion is: even a miniature steam locomotive can pull a heavy load.

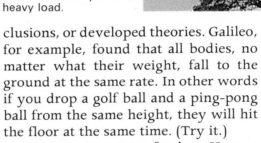

the substances our world is made of. This is the science of *chemistry*. They investigate energy and forces, in the science of *physics*. Chemistry and physics together are called the physical sciences.

Study of living things is the science of *biology*. It includes *botany*, the study of plants, and *zoology*, the study of animals. They are called the life sciences. In this book we are concerned with the physical sciences.

Do, Look and Learn

A scientist watching an apple fall from a tree would ask himself questions such as: how fast does the apple fall? Do all apples fall at the same rate? Does the rate depend on the size of the apple? Would a golf ball fall as quickly? Or a ping-pong ball? To answer these questions you will need to observe and measure – the time of fall, the height dropped, the diameter and weight of the apples, and so on.

By observing apples fall and experimenting with falling objects you will be treading in the footsteps of two of the greatest scientists the world has known – Newton and Galileo. They observed, experimented and drew con-

clusions, or developed theories. Galileo, for example, found that all bodies, no matter what their weight, fall to the ground at the same rate. In other words if you drop a golf ball and a ping-pong ball from the same height, they will hit the floor at the same time. (Try it.)

Isaac Newton went further. He saw that the force which pulls an apple to the earth is the same as that which keeps the moon in its orbit around the earth. And a similar force keeps the earth and the other planets in their orbits around the sun. He had worked out the law of gravitation.

This book describes some basic scientific facts and principles. It includes experiments you can do at home with simple equipment. Some can be done indoors on the kitchen table, others are liable to be messy so you had better do them outdoors, or in the garage or garden shed.

Safety First

Before you begin any experiment, make sure that it is safe for you and others. If an experiment involves lighting things, take care to keep inflammable materials and objects away from the flame. And make sure the matches you

strike are out before you throw them away. It is advisable to have a fire extinguisher handy, just in case of accidents. When you handle hot things, use oven gloves or tongs. If you are using chemical solutions that may be harmful to drink, keep them in stoppered bottles and label them 'poison'. Keep them in a locked cupboard so that younger children cannot reach them. Keep the equipment you use for experiments separate from the ordinary household pots and pans and bottles, or you will become unpopular with the rest of the family! And always clean up after using the equipment. A final word of warning, when you carry out electrical experiments NEVER use the house mains electricity. This can give you a severe shock and could kill you.

Being a budding scientist you will naturally want to keep a record of your experimental work. So keep a notebook, pen and pencil to jot down and sketch what you do and what the results are. Only a few of the many experiments you can do are described here. Many more can be devised to illustrate the scientific principles involved. You may well be able to think some up yourself.

The Sky by Day

WE LIVE at the bottom of a vast ocean, an ocean of air, called the atmosphere. Within this ocean, wandering currents, charged with moisture, do battle. The outcome of the battles determines our day-to-day weather. Though we can feel and hear each battle as it rages, and see its effects in the sky, we can do very little to influence its course. But we can try to understand what is happening and anticipate the next moves the warring parties may make.

The science of weather study and weather forecasting is called *meteorology*. Meteorologists collect information about the state of the atmosphere, measuring and recording the temperature, the pressure and moisture content of the air, the wind direction, and so on. From this information and their knowledge of past weather patterns, they make a guess about future weather. Today, they have computers and satellite pictures to help them, but still they cannot always make accurate forecasts. Weather is too unpredictable.

Keep a Watch on the Weather War
It is fun – and good science – to set up your own weather station. You can buy some instruments and make others (see page 12). Keep a daily record of instrument readings, and draw charts and graphs of the changes that occur. Try making your own forecasts, not only from your records, but also by reading signs that appear in the sky. See if you do as well as the weathermen.

WHY IS THE SKY BLUE?

The sun gives off white light. Space is black. Why then during the daytime is the sky blue? White light is actually a mixture of all colours – the colours of the rainbow (see page 34). When white light passes through the atmosphere, the invisible molecules of air scatter the blue light from the sun's rays. And the sky appears blue. At sunrise and sunset, however, the sun and often the whole sky turn red. This happens because the lower part of the atmosphere often contains a great deal of dust. Dust particles are bigger than air molecules; they scatter the red light from sunlight, and everything is tinged red.

The Powerhouse
The energy that drives our weather system comes from the sun. The sun's energy travels through space in the form of rays (or radiation). When they reach earth, some rays are reflected back into space by the atmosphere, the clouds and the earth's surface. But much more radiation is absorbed by the earth's surface, which heats up as a result. As it does so, it gives out heat waves. These become trapped in the atmosphere, which acts like a greenhouse and keeps the world warm.

Not all parts of the earth receive the same amount of radiation. Because the earth's surface is round, a beam of sunlight strikes different parts at different angles, and is thereby spread over greater or lesser areas. It is spread least near the equator and most near the poles. That is why the climate is, on average, hottest at the equator and becomes progressively cooler the farther you travel towards the poles. 'Climate' means the average weather conditions of a region.

Keep a Check on the Climate
Record your local temperatures over a long period at the same times each day, making sure that your thermometer is in the shade when you read it. Make a note, from the newspapers, of the

You can learn much about the weather and the nature of light by observing the sky's ever changing colours and cloud formations (left).

Make a simple shadow clock, that works like a sundial (below), by sticking a short stick into the ground. Mark the positions of the tip of the stick's shadow at different times during the course of one day. Then use the clock dial you have made to tell the time on other days.

temperatures in different cities of the world, and look up their latitudes in an atlas. See if they conform to the rule that the farther you are from the equator, the cooler it is. Do you find that inland cities are, in general, cooler or hotter than coastal cities at the same latitude?

The Path of the Sun
The sun travels through the sky in an arc, rising in the east, reaching its highest point due south (midday), and setting in the west.

As the sun moves, the colour of the sky changes, blue during the day and often red at dusk or dawn. In the morning a red sky is said to herald bad weather, whereas at night it is the 'shepherd's delight'. The panel on the page opposite will tell you what makes the colour change, but can you find

out for yourself whether the shepherds are right?

It is not the sun that moves, of course, but the earth, which spins on its axis once every 24 hours, making the sun appear to move. You can use the position of the sun to find your direction if you have a watch (see panel on page 12), but make sure you do not rely upon it on a cloudy day.

The Sun and the Seasons
The earth not only spins on its axis in space, it also travels in an orbit around the sun once a year. But its axis is tilted in space in such a way that the northern and southern hemispheres are angled more towards the sun at some times of the year than at others (see panel below). Because of this, a particular region will receive varying amounts of sun throughout

THE CHANGING SEASONS

In most places on earth, the temperature changes season by season, in a regular rhythm that affects the whole of nature. It changes because the earth's axis is tilted in space in relation to the path it follows around the sun. Because of this tilt a particular spot on earth is angled more towards the sun, and is hotter, at some times of the year than at others.

Places in the northern hemisphere are angled most towards the sun on about June 21 each year. This is their longest day and midsummer. Places in the southern hemisphere are angled most away from the sun on that date. It is their shortest day.

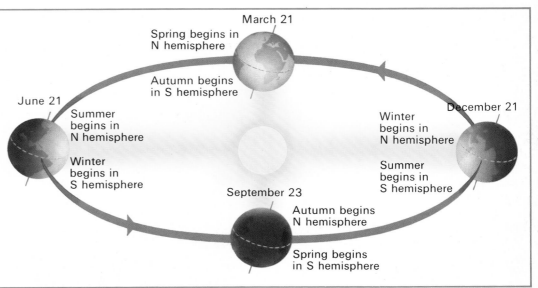

March 21
Spring begins in N hemisphere
Autumn begins in S hemisphere

June 21
Summer begins in N hemisphere
Winter begins in S hemisphere

December 21
Winter begins in N hemisphere
Summer begins in S hemisphere

September 23
Autumn begins N hemisphere
Spring begins in S hemisphere

THE WATCH COMPASS

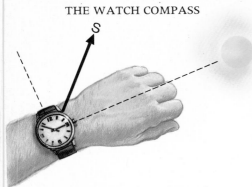

You need never be lost if you have a watch and the sun is shining, for you can use your watch as a compass. Point the hour hand of your watch at the sun, bisect (cut in two) the angle between 12 o'clock and the hour hand and you have the direction of south. The reason the watch compass works is simple. The sun travels from east to west in about 12 hours – 6 am to 6 pm. It travels 90° and is due south by 12 noon. During the same time (6–12) the hour hand of a watch travels 180°, that is, through twice as big an angle. So, by halving the angle, you are slowing down the hand to match the speed of the sun.

the year. It is this which brings about the seasons.

From earth we see the sun climb highest in the sky in summer and lowest in winter. Measure the length of the shadow of a post at midday at different times of the year and see what you find. Draw a graph showing the change in length of the shadow month by month.

The Four Winds

When sunlight strikes the earth it heats up the surface, and the air in contact with the surface heats up too. The hot air rises (see page 28), cool air comes in to take its place, and a wind is born. This happens on a world-wide scale at the equator. Air rises above the hot equatorial regions and goes north and south. Eventually it cools and sinks, and makes its way back to the equator along the surface as a wind. Other world-wide wind systems also arise because of the changes in temperature from latitude to latitude,

Rainbows appear when the sun is low in the sky behind you, and it is raining in front of you. The colour is produced when sunlight passes. through raindrops. They act as tiny prisms and split sunlight into its spectrum of individual colours (below). See also page 34.

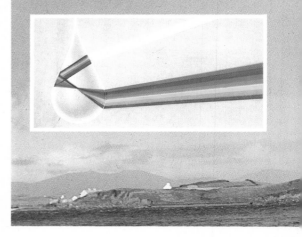

MAKING WEATHER INSTRUMENTS

You can set up a simple weather station in the garden using home-made instruments to start with. Take your instrument readings at the same times each day, if you can, and also note down the general condition of the atmosphere – cloudy, sunny, rainy, and so on.

Make a weathervane (above) by fixing a piece of plywood to the end of a wooden rod. Drill a hole through the rod and drive a nail through it into a baseboard. Mark the compass points on the board, and mount it in the right direction, on top of a pole.

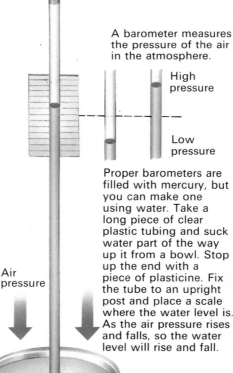

An anemometer (above) measures wind speed, 'catching' the wind in cups. Make the cups by rolling sheets of paper into cones, or use empty yoghourt cartons. Stick knitting needles through the cups with one end in a cork. Drill a hole in the middle of the cork so that it can rotate freely on a nail. Nail it to a board, with a washer or bead beneath it to reduce friction. Mount the board on a tall pole (away from trees if you can). The speed at which the anemometer spins will give you an idea of the wind speed.

Air pressure

A barometer measures the pressure of the air in the atmosphere.

High pressure

Low pressure

Proper barometers are filled with mercury, but you can make one using water. Take a long piece of clear plastic tubing and suck water part of the way up it from a bowl. Stop up the end with a piece of plasticine. Fix the tube to an upright post and place a scale where the water level is. As the air pressure rises and falls, so the water level will rise and fall.

A hygrometer measures humidity, the amount of moisture in the air. One kind is the wet and dry bulb thermometer.

Take two thermometers and wrap a piece of damp cloth around the bulb of one. Because of the cooling effect of evaporation, this thermometer should read lower than the other. The humidity of the air can be worked out from the difference between the two readings. When the humidity is low, water from the damp cloth evaporates quickly and cools the thermometer. When the humidity is high, evaporation is slower, so the difference between the two thermometer readings will be smaller.

A rain gauge measures the amount of rainfall. To make one, place a funnel in a tin can, making sure it fits so that no water enters the can round the side. If the can is exactly the same diameter as the funnel mouth, you can measure the rainfall directly with a ruler. If not, put a collecting jar inside the can and, if you are a good mathematician, you will be able to make a scale for it.

You measure wind speed with an anemometer, which has small cups that rotate in the wind. The stronger the wind blows, the faster the cups whirl round. The diagram opposite shows how to make a simple anemometer. Try making a miniature one and mounting it on the spindle of a small electric dynamo. Wire the dynamo to a galvanometer, which you can make yourself (see page 42). You will get an idea of wind speed from the amount of deflection of the galvanometer needle.

Wind speed varies greatly. A gentle breeze blows at about 15 km/h; a gale blows at more than 100 km/h. Winds of over 120 km/h are of hurricane force. But winds seldom blow steadily. Mostly they travel in a series of gusts. Gustiness is greatest during storms.

Highs and Lows
Hot air is lighter than cold air and therefore exerts less pressure. Differences in temperature over the earth's surface therefore cause differences in

spiral, rather as water spirals down a plughole. You will see evidence of this in the lines on weather charts (see page 14).

Measuring Pressure
A barometer is used to measure changes in air pressure. In a mercury barometer, the pressure of a column of mercury is balanced against the pressure of the air. When the air pressure changes, the length of the column changes. A rising barometer (pressure increasing) is a good sign, while a falling barometer (pressure decreasing) is a bad.

You can make a simple barometer using a column of water instead of mercury, to balance the air pressure (see panel opposite). The usual home barometer, however, works differently. It contains a box with much of the air removed. It is called an aneroid ('airless') barometer. The lid of the box moves in and out as the air pressure rises and falls, and works the pointer.

and further changes occur within a particular region, because of the geography. Mountain ranges, for example, force air streams to rise, and land and sea heat and cool at different rates.

A Blow by the Sea
Land heats up and cools down faster than water, and it is this which creates sea breezes. Have you noticed that there is almost always a breeze at the seaside, even though inland there may be hardly a breath of wind? During the day the land gets hotter than the sea. The air above it rises, and cool air from the sea moves inland to take its place. You get an onshore breeze. At night the land cools fast and becomes cooler than the sea. Then the air above the sea rises, and air moves from the land to take its place. You get an offshore breeze.

The Way of the Wind
It is important to know wind direction and speed, for wind carries heat, cold and moisture from place to place. You find wind direction with a weather vane. The diagram opposite shows how to make a simple one. When the wind blows, your vane will turn and point, like an arrow, to the wind direction. Remember, a wind is always named by the direction *from* which it blows – a north wind blows *from* the north.

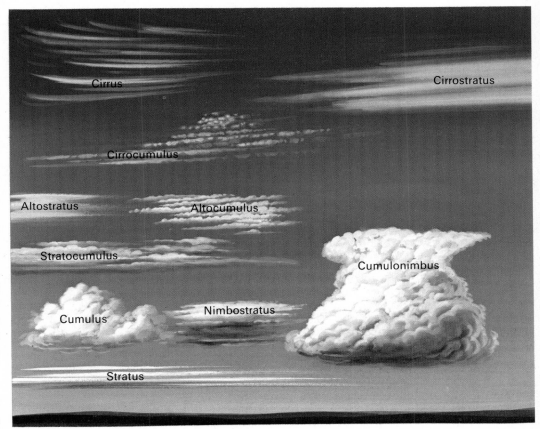

air pressure. In general, winds blow from regions of high pressure to regions of low pressure. Vast regions of high pressure (highs or anticyclones) and low pressure (lows or depressions) 'wander' over the earth's surface. Highs bring good weather; lows bring bad. Air does not move in straight lines from a high to a low but in a

Language of the Clouds
We can gain a good idea of imminent changes in the weather by watching the clouds. It is in clouds that rain, snow and hail are born. They form particularly at the boundaries (*fronts*) between air masses of different temperatures. The picture above shows the main types of clouds.

Cirrus clouds are wispy fibres that form high in the atmosphere. Often they are nicknamed 'mare's tails'. When you see them, there is almost certain to be a change in the weather. If the wisps at the ends of the 'tail' are pointing upwards, it means that the clouds are descending. Rain is on the way. If the wisps point downwards, the clouds are rising and fine weather is approaching.

Cirrus clouds may descend rapidly and grow into another kind of cloud, called *cirrocumulus*. People say that these clouds resemble the markings on a mackerel's back and that it is a 'mackerel' sky when they are about. Others merely note a sign of approaching rain.

Perhaps most familiar and most welcome are *cumulus*, the cotton-wool, or fair-weather, clouds. They drift leisurely across the summer sky and disappear at sunset. But sometimes they mass and darken to form the formidable *cumulonimbus*, the anvil-shaped thundercloud, that threatens thunder, lightning and hail.

The dark bottomed, flat *nimbostratus* is the commonest rain cloud. But *stratus* spread themselves wider, flatter and lower. They sometimes descend to within 100 metres or so of the ground.

Water Vapour

If you have walked up a hillside into low cloud, you will know what clouds are made of – fine water droplets. When water in a kettle boils, it turns into a gas–water vapour. The vapour hits the cool air and its temperature drops below boiling point. It changes back into droplets of water, which we see as steam. Clouds form in a similar way, but on a much grander scale.

Outdoors the heat from the sun turns some water from the sea and rivers into vapour. It *evaporates*. Air always contains some water vapour. When that vapour is cooled enough, it *condenses* (changes back to liquid water). In the atmosphere, the higher you go, the cooler it becomes. Air rising through the atmosphere may be cooled enough for its water vapour to condense and form clouds.

Rain, Snow and Hail

In some clouds, the water droplets move around and join up with each other to form larger drops. When the

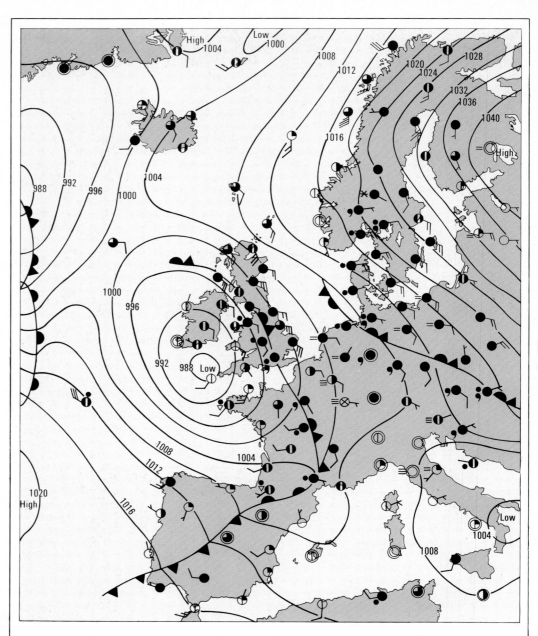

AND NOW TOMORROW'S WEATHER

Weather observers draw up charts, called synoptic charts, which show the weather pattern at a particular time. They then try to predict how this pattern will change, and issue a forecast. The chart is marked with symbols; the curving lines are isobars which show regions of similar air pressure.

CLOUD AMOUNT	GENERAL WEATHER	WIND SPEED	FRONTS
◯ 0	═ Mist	◎ Calm	Warm front
◑ 1 or less	≡ Fog		
◕ 2	❟ Drizzle	1–2 knots	Cold front
◕ 3	❟ Rain and drizzle		
◐ 4	● Rain	3–7	Occluded front
◑ 5	Rain and snow		
◕ 6	✳ Snow	8–12	Warm occlusion
◖ 7	Rain shower		
● 8	Rain and snow shower	13–17	Cold occlusion
⊗ Sky obscured	Snow shower	Add five knots for each half feather	
⊠ Missing or doubtful data	△ Hail shower		Stationary front
	⚡ Thunderstorm	48–52	

drops become heavy enough, they fall from the clouds as rain. Other clouds have ice crystals at the top, which also fall to earth when they grow large and heavy. When the lower atmosphere is warm, the crystals melt into drops and fall as rain, but when the atmosphere is cold, they remain frozen and fall as snow. Rain and snow are the commonest forms of precipitation.

In a thundercloud the crystals are tossed up and down by strong currents and do not fall until they are very large. They fall as hail. Some hailstones are the size of tennis balls but fortunately most are much smaller. If you slice a hailstone in two and examine it closely you will see that it is layered like an onion. It gains a new layer each time it is tossed upwards through the cloud.

Examine snow under a strong magnifying glass or microscope and you will see the weather's greatest wonder, a mass of exquisite six-sided ice crystals, no two of which are alike. Beautiful, too, are the feathery ice crystals that form on window-panes in winter when water vapour inside the house freezes on the cold pane. The crystals that form as frost on outdoor surfaces are much simpler in form.

Measuring Humidity

We call the amount of vapour in the atmosphere, the humidity. We can sometimes sense the humidity with our

Snow can cover the landscape in minutes (right). Snowflakes are feathery masses of tiny ice crystals in exquisite shapes. There is not as much water in snow as you might think. It takes ten centimetres of snow to make one centimetre of water. Check this for yourself by melting snow in a saucepan.

When the moisture in a room condenses on ice-cold window panes it freezes. This happens slowly and the ice that forms has time to grow into beautiful crystals like these (above).

Reading the thermometer is a regular task for the weather watcher. This one is a maximum and minimum thermometer. It contains pointers which register the highest and lowest temperatures reached over a period.

bodies. When the weather is hot and the humidity high, we feel uncomfortably hot and 'sticky'. In hot weather we keep cool by sweating. Sweat glands in the skin give off moisture which evaporates into the air and cools the skin. But when the humidity is high, the air already contains a lot of moisture. The sweat cannot evaporate quickly enough to keep us cool. So we stay hot and damp.

Humidity is measured with a hygrometer. You can make one using two thermometers, and wrapping one with a moist cloth. The two thermometers will read differently depending on the humidity (see panel on page 12). Another kind of hygrometer, the hair hygrometer, uses a bundle of human hair to absorb moisture from the air. The more humid the air, the more the hair absorbs, and the longer it gets. Try to make a simple apparatus to show this.

The Sky by Night

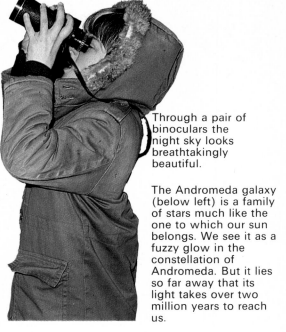

Through a pair of binoculars the night sky looks breathtakingly beautiful.

The Andromeda galaxy (below left) is a family of stars much like the one to which our sun belongs. We see it as a fuzzy glow in the constellation of Andromeda. But it lies so far away that its light takes over two million years to reach us.

WHEN you look up at the night sky, you are looking into the depths of space. The pinpoints of light which we call stars, are in reality huge suns, often bigger than our own sun. They appear as mere specks only because they are so very far away. The distance to the stars is almost too great to imagine. Even the nearest one, Proxima Centauri, lies a staggering 40 million million kilometres away. Its light takes over 4 years to reach us; it lies over 4 light-years away. But that is but a small step in space. Despite the over-awing distances involved, one can learn a lot about space simply by looking at the night sky, as astronomers have done since man first became civilized.

Use your Eyes

Astronomy is a science you can practise without any equipment at all. Using your eyes alone, you can learn to find your way about the heavens and watch the changes that take place.

The eye, however, is not an ideal optical instrument, for it can gather only a small amount of light. Its light-gathering power is limited by the size of the pupil, which is not much more than half a centimetre across even when fully open. You can get a better view of the sky with a telescope or a pair of binoculars. These have a much wider aperture (opening) than your eyes and collect much more light. They enable you to see much fainter stars. They also magnify, so that you can, for instance, make out details on the moon and the disc of some of the planets. The stars, however, are so far away that they always appear as pinpoints of light no matter how much they are magnified.

Aids to Observation

You can make a telescope quite simply from old spectacle lenses and cardboard tubing (see panel opposite). But you will have to buy your binoculars. A useful size of binoculars for star-gazing is a 7 × 50. This means that it magnifies seven times and has an aperture of 50 millimetres.

Are you Sitting Comfortably?

If you intend to spend some time observing the heavens, you will need to make a few preparations. First, you have to choose the spot from which you are going to make your observations. This should be as far as possible from house or street lights and background glare.

Since you are going to be outside standing or sitting still, you will need to wear warm clothes and, in winter, an anorak, gloves and fur-lined boots. If you are using binoculars, you will need to support them. Otherwise the stars will dance before your eyes.

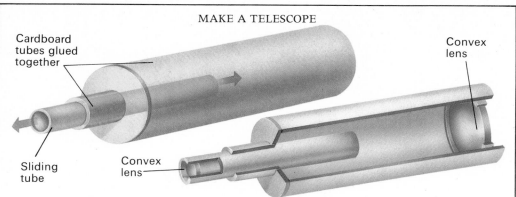

Cardboard tubes glued together

Convex lens

Sliding tube

Convex lens

You can make a refracting, or lens, telescope quite simply. You will need two cheap magnifying glasses or old spectacle lenses, which are convex (fatter in the middle), and two sturdy cardboard tubes. Fit the lenses into the tubes as shown in the picture and arrange for the eyepiece tube to move in and out so that you can focus properly. You will have to experiment to find the right places for the lenses in the tubes. The image you see with the telescope will be upside-down, but this does not matter for astronomical work.

Another kind of telescope is the reflector, which uses a curved mirror to gather light rays. This is the kind most astronomers use; they give a better optical image and can also be made much larger.

You can support binoculars simply on a pole with a crosspiece attached, or you can make a more sturdy tripod.

Find yourself a chair to sit in; a sun-lounger with arms, or a deckchair will do. To give protection from the wind, arrange some kind of screen around you, up to eye level. The windscreens you use on the beach would be fine.

Record Your Stars
Have a notebook and a torch handy so you can make sketches and notes about your observations. Clip the notebook and torch to a board, and tie a pencil to it with string. Cover the torch with a piece of red cloth or crepe paper. Dim red light has the least effect on your eyes, which, during your viewing, become adapted to the dark.

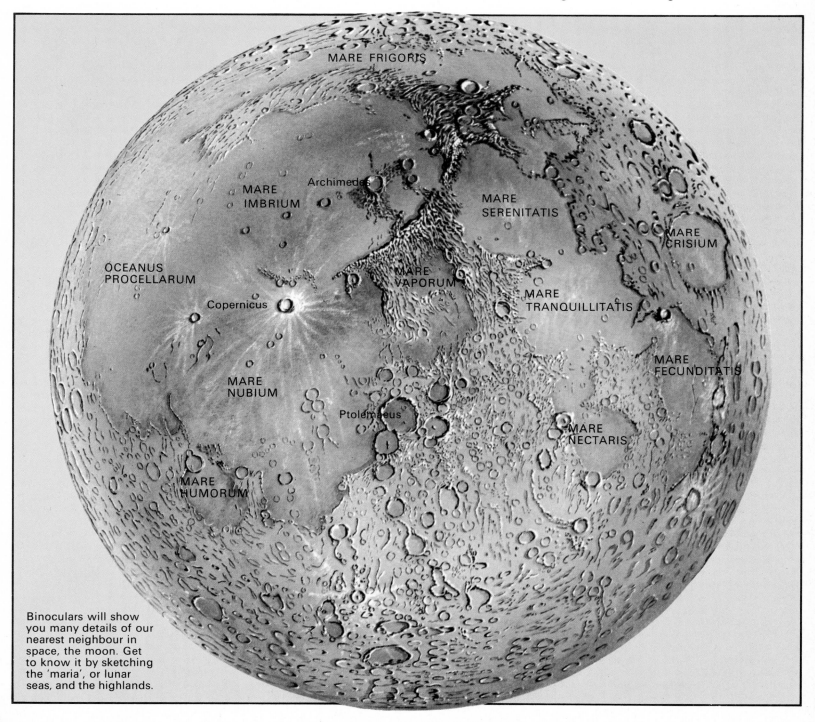

MARE FRIGORIS

MARE IMBRIUM
Archimedes

MARE SERENITATIS

MARE CRISIUM

OCEANUS PROCELLARUM

Copernicus

MARE VAPORUM

MARE TRANQUILLITATIS

MARE NUBIUM

Ptolemaeus

MARE FECUNDITATIS

MARE NECTARIS

MARE HUMORUM

Binoculars will show you many details of our nearest neighbour in space, the moon. Get to know it by sketching the 'maria', or lunar seas, and the highlands.

Other useful things to have handy are a star atlas and a clock or watch.

As you begin your observations make a note of the date and time. Always use Universal Time (UT), or Greenwich Mean Time, as all astronomers do. Remember to allow for any difference between your local time and UT, and make sure your watch is right.

Viewing conditions can affect what you see, so keep a note of them. Record whether the sky is clear, hazy or partly cloudy. Record also whether the moon is up, what phase it is at and where it is in the sky.

Observing the Moon

The moon is the earth's only natural satellite and its nearest neighbour in space. We know more about it than about any heavenly body. It is so close (about 385,000 km) that you can see some of its surface features with your

of the moon is lit, we call it a full moon. This happens a fortnight after new moon. After full moon the area of surface illuminated decreases; the moon wanes. Exactly 29½ days after one new moon, the moon disappears again at the next new moon.

You will soon notice that the moon always presents the same face to us. This is because it slowly turns on its own axis as it orbits the earth, turning once as it orbits once. Because the same side always faces us, its surface features are easy to recognize.

Signposts for Stargazers

At first glance the stars in the night sky appear to be dotted about in a random way. But as you become more familiar with the heavens, you notice that many of the bright stars form recognizable patterns; we call these patterns constellations.

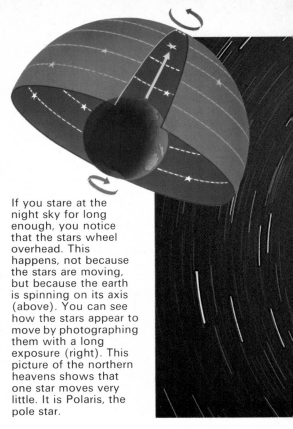

If you stare at the night sky for long enough, you notice that the stars wheel overhead. This happens, not because the stars are moving, but because the earth is spinning on its axis (above). You can see how the stars appear to move by photographing them with a long exposure (right). This picture of the northern heavens shows that one star moves very little. It is Polaris, the pole star.

A MONTH IN A FLASH It takes exactly 29½ days for the moon to complete its phases. During this time the terminator, or boundary between the light and dark areas, sweeps over the moon's surface.

You can view the lunar craters and mountains best when they are near the terminator.

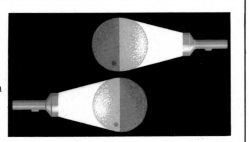

Place a ball or an orange (moon) on a table. In the dark get someone to walk around the table shining a torch on the ball. You will see the area of surface lit up change in shape just as if the moon were waxing and waning.

bare eyes. The light areas are rugged highlands and the dark areas are flat, low-lying plains. Everywhere, especially in the highlands, there are great holes, or craters.

Phases and Faces

The moon not only changes position from night to night, it also changes shape, or at least it appears to. The moon does not shine by light of its own, it merely reflects light from the sun. And as it orbits the earth, more or less of it is lit up by the sun; hence the phases we see (see panel).

At the phase of new moon, the moon is between us and the sun, and we cannot see the moon at all. A day or so later, we see the moon as a thin crescent. Then, as each day passes, more and more of the moon is lit up; the moon is waxing. When the whole face

Two of the most useful constellations for new observers are Ursa Major and Orion (see panel on page 20). The patterns their stars make are instantly recognizable. Moreover they act as invaluable signposts to other stars and constellations.

Why Does Polaris Stay Still?

The earth spins on its axis like a top. This movement gives us our day (when we are in the sun's light) and night (when we are in the earth's shadow). Polaris does not move round like the other stars because it is located almost exactly above the earth's north pole.

The spinning of the earth brings into view different stars and constellations as the night goes by. Different constellations also come into view from season to season. This is due to the earth's other motion in space, its

annual journey around the sun. As the earth travels in its orbit, its dark side (night) will face towards a different part of the heavens month by month.

How Bright are the Stars?

When you inspect the stars in the constellations more closely, you will notice that some are much brighter than others. We measure star brightness with a scale of magnitude that gives the brightest stars we can see with the naked eye the value 1 and the faintest the value 6. In a telescope or binoculars we can see much fainter stars – that is, of higher magnitude. The brightest star of all is Sirius, which can easily be found using stars in Orion as pointers.

The brightness of the stars and boundaries of the constellations are shown in star charts and atlases, essential reading for the would-be observer. Most atlases also give hints on observing and take the observer on a 'guided tour' of the most interesting features of the heavens.

Twinkle, Twinkle Little Star

The stars do not appear to shine steadily. They are constantly twinkling – haphazardly flashing bright and clear and even all colours of the rainbow. This twinkling is caused by the earth's atmosphere, not by the stars themselves.

Some stars, however, really do vary in brightness; they are called variable stars. Some change in brightness in a

few hours or a few days, others over a longer period. Your star atlas will tell you suitable variable stars to follow. You can do useful work observing and reporting the variations of variables, because professional astronomers do not have much time for such work.

You may even be lucky enough to spot a star that changes spectacularly in brightness: a nova, or new star. Novae may appear at any time, anywhere in the heavens. Looking for novae is something else that amateur astronomers can do as well as professionals.

Heavenly Wanderers

Though most stars stay in the same position in the heavens, some of the brightest seem to wander. When you train a powerful telescope on these wanderers, however, you will find that

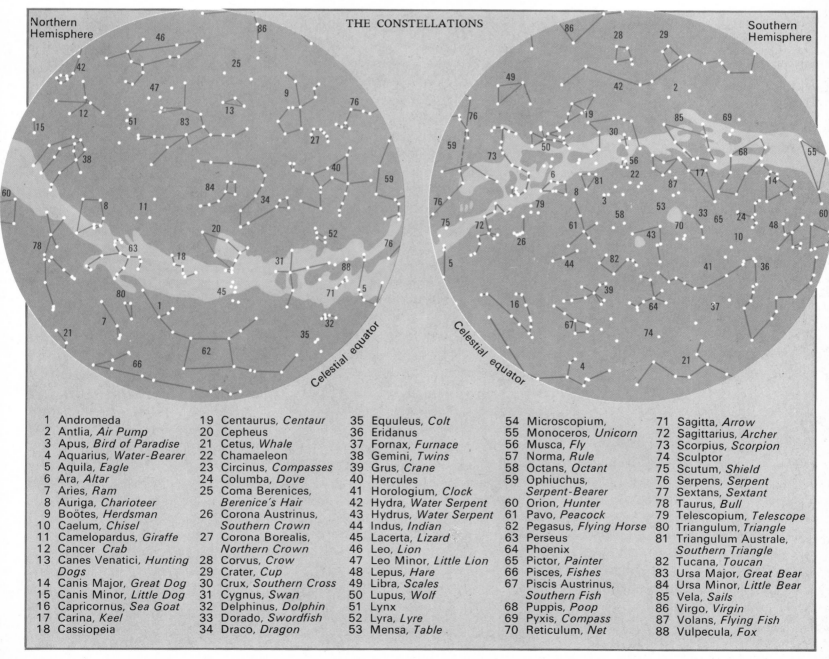

THE CONSTELLATIONS

1 Andromeda	19 Centaurus, *Centaur*	35 Equuleus, *Colt*	54 Microscopium,	71 Sagitta, *Arrow*
2 Antlia, *Air Pump*	20 Cepheus	36 Eridanus	55 Monoceros, *Unicorn*	72 Sagittarius, *Archer*
3 Apus, *Bird of Paradise*	21 Cetus, *Whale*	37 Fornax, *Furnace*	56 Musca, *Fly*	73 Scorpius, *Scorpion*
4 Aquarius, *Water-Bearer*	22 Chamaeleon	38 Gemini, *Twins*	57 Norma, *Rule*	74 Sculptor
5 Aquila, *Eagle*	23 Circinus, *Compasses*	39 Grus, *Crane*	58 Octans, *Octant*	75 Scutum, *Shield*
6 Ara, *Altar*	24 Columba, *Dove*	40 Hercules	59 Ophiuchus,	76 Serpens, *Serpent*
7 Aries, *Ram*	25 Coma Berenices,	41 Horologium, *Clock*	*Serpent-Bearer*	77 Sextans, *Sextant*
8 Auriga, *Charioteer*	*Berenice's Hair*	42 Hydra, *Water Serpent*	60 Orion, *Hunter*	78 Taurus, *Bull*
9 Boötes, *Herdsman*	26 Corona Austrinus,	43 Hydrus, *Water Serpent*	61 Pavo, *Peacock*	79 Telescopium, *Telescope*
10 Caelum, *Chisel*	*Southern Crown*	44 Indus, *Indian*	62 Pegasus, *Flying Horse*	80 Triangulum, *Triangle*
11 Camelopardus, *Giraffe*	27 Corona Borealis,	45 Lacerta, *Lizard*	63 Perseus	81 Triangulum Australe,
12 Cancer *Crab*	*Northern Crown*	46 Leo, *Lion*	64 Phoenix	*Southern Triangle*
13 Canes Venatici, *Hunting*	28 Corvus, *Crow*	47 Leo Minor, *Little Lion*	65 Pictor, *Painter*	82 Tucana, *Toucan*
Dogs	29 Crater, *Cup*	48 Lepus, *Hare*	66 Pisces, *Fishes*	83 Ursa Major, *Great Bear*
14 Canis Major, *Great Dog*	30 Crux, *Southern Cross*	49 Libra, *Scales*	67 Piscis Austrinus,	84 Ursa Minor, *Little Bear*
15 Canis Minor, *Little Dog*	31 Cygnus, *Swan*	50 Lupus, *Wolf*	*Southern Fish*	85 Vela, *Sails*
16 Capricornus, *Sea Goat*	32 Delphinus, *Dolphin*	51 Lynx	68 Puppis, *Poop*	86 Virgo, *Virgin*
17 Carina, *Keel*	33 Dorado, *Swordfish*	52 Lyra, *Lyre*	69 Pyxis, *Compass*	87 Volans, *Flying Fish*
18 Cassiopeia	34 Draco, *Dragon*	53 Mensa, *Table*	70 Reticulum, *Net*	88 Vulpecula, *Fox*

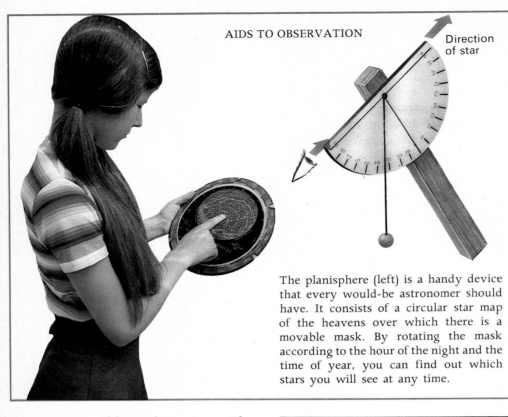

Direction of star

You can be more scientific about your observations of stars and planets if you measure their position in the sky and note how this changes from night to night and from season to season. These drawings will help you to make a simple alidade (left) and theodolite (below).

The alidade enables you to measure the angle of a star above the horizon. The theodolite gives you the star's direction as well. It has an alidade mounted on an arm that can swing round the compass points.

Direction of star

The planisphere (left) is a handy device that every would-be astronomer should have. It consists of a circular star map of the heavens over which there is a movable mask. By rotating the mask according to the hour of the night and the time of year, you can find out which stars you will see at any time.

they are not like other stars. They present a distinct disc, not a pinpoint of light. They are in fact planets, bodies like the earth which orbit the sun. Three of the planets are unmistakable. Venus is the brightest object in the night sky, after the moon. For much of the year it shines brilliantly in the western sky at sunset, when we call it the evening star. At other times we can see it in the eastern sky at sunrise as the morning star. Sometimes rivalling Venus in brightness is the giant planet Jupiter. The third and most distinctive of all is Mars, shining with a fiery reddish-orange hue.

Though you cannot make out any details on the planets' discs with only a small telescope or binoculars, you can chart their progress through the sky month by month, and note how their brightness changes.

The Milky Way

On a really dark, moonless night you can see a faint hazy band arching across the heavens. This is the Milky Way. Examine it with binoculars and you will find that it is made up of millions of stars, packed closely together. It is a slice through the galaxy to which all the stars we can see belong. Our galaxy (it is only one of many) is thought to contain about 100,000 million stars. Of these, many are similar in size and brightness to the sun; some are far smaller and dimmer; others are far larger and brighter.

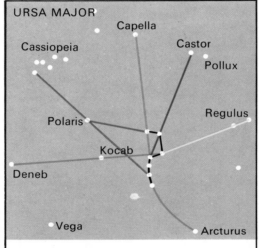

URSA MAJOR

Capella
Cassiopeia
Castor
Pollux
Polaris
Regulus
Kocab
Deneb
Vega
Arcturus

KEY CONSTELLATIONS

Ursa Major and Orion are among the most unmistakable constellations in the heavens. And they are two of the observer's best friends, for they enable him to find other stars and constellations that are more difficult to locate. The diagrams show how useful they are. The end two stars in the ploughshare (in Ursa Major) are particularly valuable because they point to the pole star. They are known as the pointers.

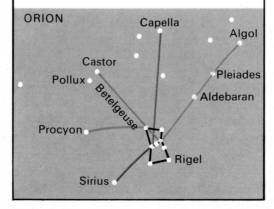

ORION

Capella
Algol
Castor
Pollux
Pleiades
Betelgeuse
Aldebaran
Procyon
Rigel
Sirius

A great many stars travel through space with a companion. Star atlases will tell you where you can see examples of these double stars. Some stars cluster together in large groups. Most unmistakable is the group called the Pleiades, or Seven Sisters (see picture).

As well as single stars and star groups, the galaxy contains shining clouds of gas and dust called nebulae. If you look below the three stars that form Orion's Belt, you will see the most prominent nebula of all, the Great Nebula in Orion.

If you look in the constellation Andromeda, you will also see a misty patch that appears to be a nebula. But it is not a nebula in our galaxy, but another galaxy altogether. It is so far away that its light takes over 2 million years to reach us and it appears like a mere puff of dust.

Cosmic Dust and Pebbles

The planets and their moons are the main bodies in the sun's family, or solar system. But there are also many minor bodies. The biggest are the asteroids, rocky lumps which orbit the sun between Mars and Jupiter. You cannot see them in ordinary telescopes because they are too small and too far away.

Other rocky debris does make its presence felt, however. Every night, if you remain stargazing for long enough you will see streaks of light

Always keep a look out for comets — enormous streamers of glowing gas and dust. The photograph (left) shows Comet West, which broke into pieces in 1975.

HALLEY'S COMET

The most famous of all comets is named after the British astronomer Sir Edmond Halley. It was the comet seen at the Battle of Hastings in 1066 and appears on the Bayeux Tapestry. Halley's comet last appeared in 1910 and is due again in 1986/7.

The Pleiades (left) is a bright cluster of young stars in the constellation of Taurus, the Bull. If your eyesight is keen, you may be able to see all seven of its brightest stars. These earn it the nickname, 'Seven Sisters'.

The giant planet Jupiter (right), photographed through a powerful telescope. Jupiter is eleven times bigger across than the earth. It lies on average about 800 million kilometres away. The bands you see in the picture are belts of cloud in Jupiter's thick atmosphere.

which look almost like stars falling from the sky. These streaks, often called shooting stars or falling stars, are meteors. They appear when lumps of rock hurtle into the earth's atmosphere from outer space and burn up in the heat produced by air friction. Count the number of meteors you can see in an hour. Does this number vary from month to month?

Occasionally, meteoric lumps are big enough to survive their passage through the atmosphere, and reach the ground intact. Then they are called meteorites. Some are stony, others are made up of iron and nickel. Particularly large meteor lumps create fireballs. These announce their presence with a whoosh, a supersonic bang and a vivid coloured trail. If you happen to see one, note down the time and direction in which it was moving, and telephone the details to your local astronomical society. From several such observations its path can be plotted, and the place where it fell can be found.

Another kind of 'shooting star' is the comet. This is a mass of dust and frozen gas which starts to glow as it approaches the sun. The sun's heat melts some of the gas and releases dust. This fans out from the head of the comet to form a fainter tail. The tail always points away from the sun because it is swept away by the stream of particles constantly given off by the sun. Several comets appear every year, but few of them are very bright. You may find one yourself. If you are the first to report it, it will be named after you, and your reputation as an astronomer will be made.

Up Hill and Down Dale

STUDYING the earth's crust and the changes that take place in it is the science of *geology*. As well as observing the landscape generally, geologists often take samples of exposed rock formations. Within the rocks they may find deposits of minerals, some in the form of colourful crystals. Collecting rocks and minerals is a good way to start studying geology.

You can find rock samples practically everywhere, not only in the mountains, but in the garden and on the roadside; on the river bank and seashore, and on construction sites. At the seaside the action of the sea will have split off rock samples for you and rounded them into smooth lumps. Elsewhere you will probably need a hammer to break off samples. A geological hammer is best – it has a square head at one end and a chisel point at the other. The panel on the opposite page will show you what else you may need.

At the seaside do not be too adventurous. Keep away from cliff faces, especially if they overhang, for rocks may suddenly split off and fall on you. Also watch the tide, which can come in suddenly and cut off your retreat. Whenever you take a sample, label it and record where you took it. You may also wish to sketch interesting features of the location.

Recognize the Rocks

Buy yourself a good field guide to rocks and take it with you on your rock-hunting expeditions. You will soon learn to recognize common rocks, such as granite and chalk. These are examples of the two main types of rock. Granite is an *igneous* rock, formed of hot molten rock (magma) from the earth's interior that pushed itself up to the surface and gradually cooled.

Chalk, by contrast, started out in the sea. A clue to its origins can be found by grinding it to powder and examining it under a microscope. You will find it is made up of tiny shells, the remains, or fossils, of microscopic creatures that lived in the sea millions of years ago.

The result of millions of years of erosion, Cedar Breaks canyon in Utah in the United States, forms a huge and spectacular panorama (left).

Molten rock from deep inside the earth forces its way through weaknesses in the crust to form a volcano (below). Not even the sea can damp down its dramatic exhibition.

As these creatures died, their shells (made of the mineral calcium carbonate) dropped to the sea floor and piled up as layers of sediment. Millions of years passed and the sediment became very thick and compressed into the soft rock we know as chalk. We call it a *sedimentary*, or bedded rock.

Among other common sedimentary rocks are limestone, sandstone, and shale. Sandstone consists of grains of sand cemented together. Seaside beaches are sandstone in the making.

Plants can split rocks apart. Seeds settle in crevices in the rock and begin to grow. The roots exert greater and greater pressure inside the crevices until the rock splits (below).

Obsidian (Igneous rock)

Basalt Igneous rock)

Shale is formed when mud is compressed into rock. See how fine and smooth it is compared with sandstone. Limestones are mostly calcium carbonate. Some are formed like chalk from fossil shells. You can sometimes see the fossils. But in other types you can see none. These limestones were formed when water containing dissolved calcium carbonate evaporated. The 'fur' in a kettle forms in a similar way. Every time you heat the kettle some of the water evaporates and tiny specks of the calcium carbonate it contains come out of solution when it cools.

Weathering Heights
Calcium carbonate gets into water as a result of weathering. Weathering is one form of *erosion*. Rain, wind, sun and frost launch a combined attack that will eventually reduce even the highest peaks to humble hillocks. Rain batters rocks and loosens the minerals they contain. It also contains chemicals absorbed from the air which attack the rock.

Mites and Tites
Calcium carbonate in particular is easily dissolved. Streams running through chalk and limestone hills cut deep channels as they dissolve the rock. Often they bore their way downwards through the rock layers, or strata and form underground caverns and tunnels. In many of them great pillars hang from the roof (stalactites) and rise from the floor (stalagmites). These are formed by the constant dripping of mineral-laden water.

Shattered by Sun and Frost
The combined effect of sun and frost can be seen at the foot of any rock face as a pile of rock chips called scree. In the heat of the sun rock expands; at night it cools and contracts. This sets up stresses in the rock which eventually cause it to shatter. When water gets into crevices in the rock and freezes, it expands and forces the rock apart like a wedge.

Cut by Water
Running water is one of the most powerful agents of erosion. Notice how rivulets form in earthy banks after a rainstorm. You can see similar channels bored in the rock on mountainsides. Water in these channels

When you are exploring a rocky site, jot down, or sketch, any interesting features so that you can remember them later. You may like to photograph particularly interesting sites for your records.

carries along rock chips and pebbles which help to grind away the rocks they come into contact with. The Grand Canyon in the United States is a result of millions of years of erosion by the Colorado River. The river bed lies over $1\frac{1}{2}$ kilometres beneath the canyon rim and is still dropping. Even if you cannot visit such a spectacular canyon, you can still see many deep gorges and valleys. Look at the layers and layers of rocks and imagine the millions of years they took to build, the millions of fossil shells that went into them, and the millions of years it has taken to wear them away.

Ground by Glaciers
Rock layers can also be seen in valleys carved by glaciers during the ice ages. Though made up of solid ice, a glacier moves slowly downhill. Embedded within it are rocks and pebbles which grind the sides and floor of the valley as the glacier moves.

Record of the Rocks
Geologists assume that normally the lower layers of rock were deposited earlier than the layers above them.

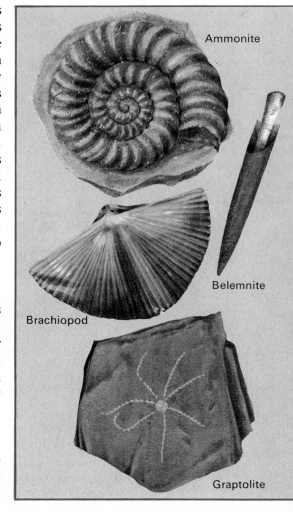

Ammonite

Belemnite

Brachiopod

Graptolite

24

It is worth looking closely at nodules of flint (left), for they are often studded with fossils.

In a few million years, these shells on a sandy beach (right) will be changed into rock. The photograph of limestone (below) shows the chalky fossils of which it is made.

A fallen tree in Arizona (right), its trunk shattered into chunks — not of wood but of solid rock. Petrified wood is formed by water seeping into the trunk of a dead tree and depositing minerals in place of the decayed plant fibres. Over millions of years, the minerals harden into solid rock, forming a perfect fossil.

Interesting fossils, such as these (below), can be found in most bedded rocks. Only rarely do you come across the remains of huge creatures like dinosaurs.

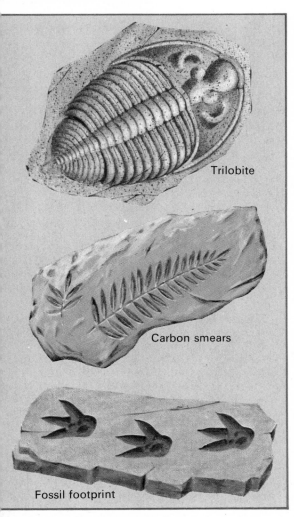

Trilobite

Carbon smears

Fossil footprint

From the layers they can build up a picture of how the earth has changed over millions of years. They have divided up past geological time into eras, periods and epochs, just as we divide everyday time into years, days and hours. The names of these are difficult to remember but it is as well to learn them as soon as you can.

Trapped within the rock layers geologists find fossils of the creatures that once teemed in the seas, or roamed the land. From the position of the fossils in the layers, they can tell in what order the creatures inhabited the earth and approximately when. Collecting and studying fossils is the science of *palaeontology*.

Finding Fossils

You are bound to come across plenty of fossils on your travels, especially in chalk and limestone hills. In sandstone, the rock formed from ancient beaches, look for fossil footprints of seashore birds and other creatures. Look also for ripple marks made by the lapping waves of an ancient sea. The currents of that sea also have left their signature in the rocks in what appear to be layers

at an angle to the normal strata. This is called current bedding.

Minerals

All rocks are made up of chemical substances called minerals. The amounts of the minerals in a particular type of rock can vary widely. Two specimens of granite, for example, will contain different amounts of felspar, quartz and mica. This is how rocks differ from minerals. A mineral has a composition that never varies from specimen to specimen. Quartz, for example, always contains one atom of silicon to every two atoms of oxygen. Its chemical name is silicon dioxide, or silica.

Quartz not only occurs in rocks mixed with other minerals, but often can be found by itself in cavities inside the rocks. There it may form beautiful six-sided, pointed crystals, often used as gemstones. Agate and onyx are other forms of quartz which are opaque, but beautifully marked and coloured.

Beautiful crystals are hard to find. But silica can be easily found in more common guises, such as reddish-yellow grains of sand. In chalk it occurs as lumps of flint.

All that Glitters

Silica is not the only mineral that appears in various guises. If you think you have found a lump of gold, check first that you have not been fooled by iron pyrites. This often occurs as yellow metallic lumps and is nicknamed fool's gold. The zinc mineral blende is named sphalerite ('deceiver') because it often resembles the more valuable lead mineral galena. The iron mineral haematite is sometimes found as shiny rounded lumps and named 'kidney' ore, or as tiny grey mirror-like crystals, named 'looking-glass' ore. (You will often come across the word 'ore' when reading about minerals. Ores are minerals which can be processed in furnaces to obtain a metal).

As you will find from experience, appearances in the mineral world are deceptive. Only in a few cases (for example the beautiful copper minerals

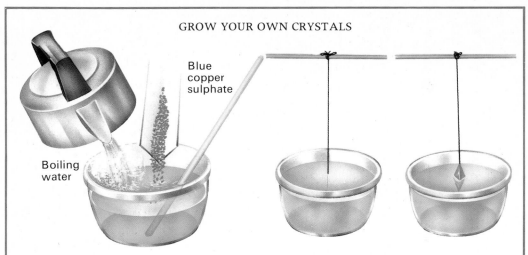

GROW YOUR OWN CRYSTALS

Blue copper sulphate

Boiling water

Under the right conditions minerals grow into beautiful crystals of many different shapes and sizes and colours. You can grow crystals easily yourself, using common minerals found in the home and garden, such as washing soda, table salt and Epsom salts.

Pour hot water into a heat-proof dish or beaker and add the mineral little by little, stirring all the time until it dissolves. Eventually you will find that the solution becomes saturated – no more mineral will dissolve. Now allow the solution to cool. As it does so, the mineral will start to come out of solution as crystals. To encourage crystals to form dangle a thread in the solution, and the crystals will form on the end.

HOW HARD IS IT?

The *hardness* of minerals is usually expressed on a scale that goes from the softest mineral, talc (1) to the hardest mineral, diamond (10). If you can scratch your mineral specimen with a fingernail, its hardness is about 2; with a bronze coin, 3; with glass, 4; with a penknife, 5; with flint, 6; and with a hard steel file, 7.

The rocks that form the earth's crust are made up of thousands of different minerals. Many are very colourful and form beautifully shaped crystals. The finest sparkle as gems in rings, necklaces and other jewellery. Beside them, other minerals often look dull and uninteresting. But they can be important. Many are ores – minerals which can be processed into metals. Others are used to make invaluable items, such as bricks, pottery and cement.

1

2

3

4

8

9

10

deep-blue azurite and emerald-green malachite) are minerals instantly recognizable by their crystal shape or colour. In general you must apply other identification tests.

One characteristic is lustre, the way a mineral reflects light. A mineral may have a metallic sheen, or look silky, pearly or dull. Another characteristic property is hardness (see panel).

Minerals also differ in the way they break, or fracture. Mica has the distinctive property of cleavage. It splits into thin, flaky parallel sheets. Flint breaks into oval razor-sharp flakes when struck.

When rubbed on a tile or stiff paper, many minerals leave a coloured streak that helps identify them. Haematite, for example, leaves a cherry red streak; pyrites leaves a greenish black streak.

The relative density, or specific gravity (SG) of a mineral is also characteristic. Some minerals feel particularly heavy. Barytes, for example, often looks like calcite or quartz but is immediately distinguished because it is twice as heavy.

Minerals may be distinguished from each other by the different ways they react when treated with acid. Pour acid on to quartz and nothing happens. Pour acid on to calcite and the surface of the mineral starts to fizz. The acid is attacking the calcite (calcium carbonate) and carbon dioxide gas is bubbling off. The same test distinguishes limestone (also calcium carbonate) from sandstone (silica).

Finding out what a mineral is can turn into quite an involved process. But it is good scientific detective work. You will need a good field guide to give you details. Remember to take notes on what you do and label your collection for the benefit of everyone.

As your rock collection grows, it becomes important to keep accurate records. Label your samples with their common and scientific names, and the place where you found them. With a little imagination, you can make an attractive display of them (above).

Some rocks that look alike can be distinguished by the acid test (left). Rocks such as chalk and limestone fizz when acid is poured on them.

1 Geode filled with amethyst crystals
2 Smithsonite
3 Galena
4 Wavellite
5 Kidney iron ore
6 Fluorite, or fluorspar
7 Malachite
8 'Dog-tooth' calcite
9 Ziosite with ruby
10 Realgar
11 Dolomite with iron pyrites
12 Sulphur

Air, Fire and Water

You can show how strong air pressure is in a number of ways. Place a wooden ruler on the edge of a table so that part of it sticks out (left).
Cover the rest with a sheet of newspaper and smooth it down. Now strike the end of the ruler sharply and see if the paper will lift. Could the pressure of the air on the newspaper possibly be stronger than a blow from your fist?

Pour a jugful of water into an empty oil can (right), and heat the can on the stove with the lid off (inset). When steam comes from the spout, take the can off the stove and quickly screw the lid back on. (WEAR OVEN GLOVES TO DO THIS.) Take the can outside and pour cold water over it. As the steam inside cools, the can will crumple up. The cooling steam will have created a vacuum inside, which cannot withstand the air pressure outside.

WE CANNOT see it, taste it or smell it, but it is all around us and we can feel it when it moves. It is the air, which breathes life into our planet. Movements of the air masses around the earth bring about changes in weather. What makes the air move? The heat from the sun does. The sun does not heat the air directly. It heats the ground and the ground heats the air above it. What happens when air is heated? It expands. You can easily show this by stretching a balloon over the neck of an empty milk bottle. The balloon hangs limply down. Put the bottle in a saucepan of water and heat up the water. The air in the bottle expands as it heats and gradually inflates the balloon.

Hot Up and Cold Down

When air expands, it becomes lighter, or less dense than the air around it. Being lighter, it rises, just as a cork (which is lighter than water) rises when you release it underwater. When air becomes colder it sinks. Open a refrigerator door, and your toes will soon get colder as the cold air pours out on to the floor.

Rising and descending columns of hot and cold air dominate the weather pattern of the earth. Pressure beneath an ascending column is lower than that beneath a descending column.

The Weight of Air

Air pressure is the force exerted on everything on earth by the weight of air above it. You are yourself supporting between 5000 and 6000 kilograms of air — about 1 kilogram on every square centimetre of your body. You do not feel weighed down because the pressures above and below you balance out. Because air pressure depends on the amount of air above you, the higher you climb above sea level, the lower the air pressure becomes.

Low air pressure is the reason behind the answer to a favourite quiz question, 'Why can't you make a good pot of tea

on Mt Everest?' On Mt Everest, over 8800 metres high, the air pressure is very low. And because it is low, water boils at a much lower temperature than it does at sea level, so it does not extract as much flavour from the tea leaves.

The Power of Pressure

Try the experiments shown in the photographs on these pages and you will soon realize how strong air pres-

PUT OUT THE LIGHT

Nothing can burn without oxygen. That is why the quickest way to put out a fire is to cover it and exclude the air. A simple experiment enables you to find out roughly how much oxygen there is in the air. Light a candle and stand it in a shallow bowl of water. Quickly place over it a bottle or jar, with the mouth of the bottle below the surface of the water. As the candle burns, the oxygen in the bottle will be used up, and the water will gradually rise in the neck of the bottle to take its place. Soon the candle will go out, showing that all the oxygen has gone. Note the level of the water in the bottle and on the candle, and then remove the bottle.

You can now find out what volume of water was sucked into the bottle. Remember to allow for the volume of the candle. To find the volume of the bottle minus the candle, fill it with water and stick in the candle to the level it was during the experiment. Some water will spill over. Pour the rest into a measuring jug and note its volume. Now, keeping the candle in position, pour water in the bottle until it reaches the level reached (the other way up) in the experiment. Measure that volume. The difference in volume will give you the volume of oxygen in the bottle. It should be about one fifth of the total volume. Is it?

With air pressure to help you, you can turn a glass of water upside down without spilling it. Fill a glass with water and place a flat card over it (left top). Holding the card in place, turn the glass upside down, then take your hand away. The air presses against the card, keeping the water in the glass.

Have you got strong lungs? Then try blowing over a pile of books. Blowing in the ordinary way (right top), you cannot do it. You can do it however with a simple trick. Place a plastic bag flat under the bottom book, so that the mouth protrudes. Now blow into the bag, and you will find that the pressure of air in the bag lifts the books and makes them topple over. The pressure builds up into a strong enough force because it is spread over a large area.

Try blowing apart two apples hanging side by side. Instead of moving apart, the apples actually move together (left). The explanation for this is that as you increase the speed of the air (by blowing), you reduce its pressure. So the surrounding air has greater pressure and pushes the apples together.

Siphoning (right) is a useful way of transferring liquid from one jar to another with the least disturbance. For the siphon to work, the liquid level in the receiving jar must be lower than that in the other. You start the siphoning action by sucking at the lower end of the siphon tube.

sure is. In the first, it makes a newspaper appear stronger than wood, but this is not surprising if you calculate the force of air pressing on the whole newspaper. Remember *total force = pressure × area*.

The second experiment shows how you can turn a glass of water upside down without spilling it. This experiment would still work if you did it with a glass up to 10 metres deep! That is the height of the column of water which the air can support. The third experiment, featuring the oil can, shows vividly and noisily the crushing effect of air pressure. Be careful when you attempt it. Not all cans are suitable. The fourth experiment shows how you can make air work for you and trick your friends.

Blowing Apples

Another simple experiment demonstrates the principle behind aeroplane flight. Try blowing further apart two apples that are dangling on strings a few centimetres apart. You cannot do it. Far from moving apart, they actually move closer together! If the apples move together, then the air on the outside must press them inwards. Blowing must have reduced the air pressure between the apples. By blowing, you increase the speed of the air. When you increase the speed of air, you decrease its pressure. A scientist named Daniel Bernoulli first found this out two centuries ago, and it is called Bernoulli's Law.

An aeroplane can fly because of the shape of its wings. The wings are curved at the top and flat at the bottom. Air passing over the curved top moves faster than the air passing beneath, so pressure is lower above than beneath. The wing therefore tends to lift into the low-pressure region.

Burning Nails

Leave a shiny new iron nail in the air for some time and it rusts. Something in the air affects the iron chemically. In fact, it is the oxygen in the air. Oxygen makes up about a fifth of the air by volume. When something burns in air, it combines with the oxygen: it oxidises. Burning is one form of oxidation, rusting is another. The latter is a very slow process, whereas burning is very fast. The chemical name of rust on iron is iron oxide.

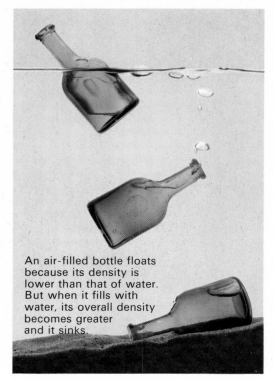

An air-filled bottle floats because its density is lower than that of water. But when it fills with water, its overall density becomes greater and it sinks.

The general term for the attack on metals by air and other chemicals is corrosion. Each metal is affected differently. Whereas iron corrodes readily, aluminium and copper do not. Leave a selection of different metals outside for several months. Try iron, steel, tin, lead, copper, bronze and 'silver' coins, aluminium, zinc (from old dry battery cases), galvanized wire, and anything else you can find. Make a note of which ones corrode and the form the corrosion takes. Why does painting protect metals?

Corrosion is worse in damp weather because moisture is needed to help it along. It is also worse in industrial areas where the atmosphere is polluted with acid gases. The gases dissolve in the water vapour in the atmosphere and eventually fall as acid rain. This acid speeds up the corrosion process. The

Stubble flaming in a field (left) and iron rusting in a farmyard (below) may seem totally different, but they are not. They are different examples of the same thing — burning. Fire is fast burning, rusting is slow burning. In each case the substance is combining with oxygen in the air to form an oxide. The stubble changes to carbon dioxide and the iron to iron oxide, or rust.

Both water and oxygen are needed to make iron rust. If you put iron nails in water which contains no air, no rusting occurs. Use oil or wax to exclude air in your experiment (right).

DECOMPOSING WATER

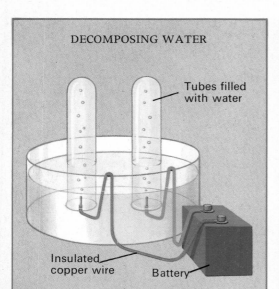

Tubes filled with water

Insulated copper wire

Battery

Water is a chemical compound made up of hydrogen and oxygen. Using electricity (not from the mains) you can break water down into its constituents. Fill a dish with water and add to it a few tablespoonfuls of vinegar. (This makes water a better conductor of electricity.) Attach wires to a battery, or several batteries joined together to give more power, and dip the ends in the water. Bubbles will soon start to rise from the wires as the electricity decomposes the water into hydrogen and oxygen.

Collect the gas given off by upturning test-tubes full of water over the wires. The gas will gradually displace the water and collect in the tubes. After a while you will notice that one tube contains much more gas than the other. Remove the tube and hold a lighted match to its mouth. A loud 'plop' will tell you that the gas is hydrogen. Remove the second tube and test the gas there with a glowing splint. This should burst into flames, telling you that it is oxygen.

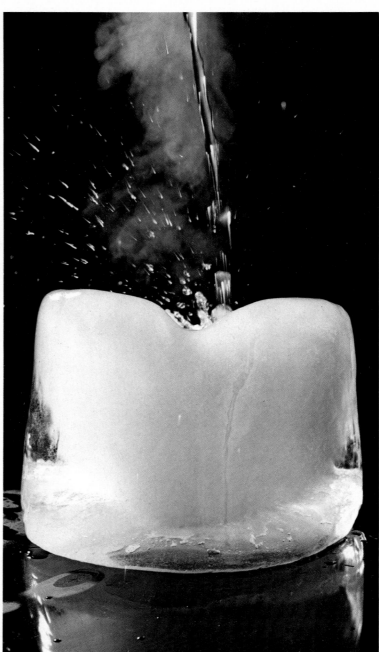

Every substance exists at room temperature in one of three states. It is either a solid, a liquid, or a gas. But if the temperature changes, the substance can change its state. Suppose that a substance is normally a liquid. Then, if you cool it enough, it turns into a solid. If you heat it enough, it turns into a gas. The picture (left) shows the three states of water. Hot water in its normal liquid state is being poured on to a lump of ice, which is water in its frozen solid state. Rising above the melting ice is steam, which is water in its gaseous state.

Fill a bottle with water. Put it in a plastic bag and leave it in the freezer. As the water freezes it will expand and break the bottle. Water expanding into ice can burst water pipes in winter.

salt spread on icy roads also increases corrosion in car bodies. The salty water forms little electric cells on the steel, which cause it to be eaten away. This form of corrosion is called electro-chemical (see page 43).

Water, Water Everywhere
Water covers more than 70 per cent of the earth's surface. It is one of the commonest minerals and the only one which is found native in the liquid state. It is one of the best solvents known – it will dissolve a wide variety of substances. Sea water contains a large number of dissolved minerals, mainly common salt (sodium chloride).

Have you noticed that the sea hardly ever freezes, even when freshwater ponds nearby are frozen solid? One reason for this is the salt. When you dissolve something in a liquid, you

THE CARTESIAN DIVER

An interesting toy to make is the Cartesian diver, which you can cause to bob up and down through the water like a miniature submarine. Fill a large jar with water and place, upside-down, inside it a miniature liqueur bottle partly filled with water so that it just floats. Tie a thin rubber sheet (old balloon) over the neck of the jar so that there is no air trapped beneath it. Press the sheet with the palm of your hand and the liqueur bottle will begin to sink. Release the pressure, and your 'diver', or bottle-imp, as it is sometimes called, will obediently return to the surface.

lower the temperature at which it freezes. This is why sea water freezes at a lower temperature than fresh water; why salt is applied to icy roads; and why antifreeze is added to the water-cooling system of a car.

Why do we need to prevent the water in a car engine from freezing? To find the answer, fill an unwanted glass bottle with water, stopper it tightly and tie it inside a plastic bag. Then put it into the freezing compartment of the refrigerator overnight. See what has happened in the morning.

Drop an egg into a glass of water and it will sink. It will sink because it is heavier, or denser, than water. But with the help of salt, you can make the egg float. Shake the salt into the water and stir, so that it dissolves.

Keep adding salt and you will find that the egg will eventually begin to rise from the bottom and float. By adding the salt you increase the density of the water until it is greater than that of the egg. When this happens, the egg floats.

The Pressure of Water

Just as air exerts pressure, so does water. You can feel the water pressing against your eardrums when you dive deep under water. As you would expect, the water pressure increases with depth. To demonstrate this, punch holes down the side of an empty oil can and fill it with water. The jet from the bottom hole will be strongest, indicating that the pressure at the bottom of the can is greatest. Measure the distance of each hole from the surface of the water and the distance the jets of water reach. Plot a graph showing the relationship between them.

Divers and Drivers

Because water is so much denser than air, it exerts far greater pressure. When men venture into the ocean depths, they have to wear strong steel diving suits. For every 10 metres you descend into the water, the pressure increases by 1 atmosphere (1 kilogram per square cm). The deep-diving craft Trieste descended to one of the deepest parts of the Pacific Ocean in 1960, reaching a depth of 10·9 kilometres. Calculate what the pressure on it was.

You can make an interesting little diver yourself, which works because of differences in the way gases and liquids behave (see panel). It is called a Cartesian diver, after the French philosopher René Descartes. The diver bobs up and down because gases are compressible while liquids are incompressible. When you press down on the top of the jar, water, which cannot be compressed, is forced into the 'diver', compressing the air inside. The bottle thus becomes heavier and sinks.

You would get the same result if you scaled up the experiment and placed the diver anywhere in a large tank of water. This is because liquids transmit pressure equally in all directions.

Many devices depend for their action on the transmission of pressure through liquids. They are called hydraulic devices. The foot brakes of a car are hydraulic. Find out how they work and how the force the driver applies to the brake pedal is magnified to operate the brakes. (Remember again that *force = pressure × area*.)

Eureka!

One of the best known stories in science concerns the ancient Greek scientist Archimedes, who thought of the scientific principle named after him as he stepped into a full bath. He noticed as he did so that the bath overflowed. His body had displaced a certain weight of water. He realized that this weight was equal to the weight he apparently lost when he stepped into the bath. He was so excited, so the story goes, that he rushed naked into the street crying 'Eureka!' ('I have found it.'). By applying this principle he was able to discover that someone was diluting the gold in his king's crown.

You need not climb in and out of baths to illustrate his principle. One simple way is to weigh objects that float in water without using scales. Try weighing an apple, for example. Fill a large jug to the brim with water and place a small measuring jug beneath the spout. Carefully place your apple in the large jug. Water will spill over into the small jug. The weight of water that overflows equals the weight of the apple (it has lost all its weight). Read the weight (in grams) of the apple from the scale on the jug, which will be marked in cubic centimetres (1 cc of water weighs 1 gram).

When you dip one corner of a lump of sugar in your tea, the liquid rapidly rises into the lump. This is the result of capillary action — the tendency of liquids to rise in narrow tubes. In a sugar lump there are tiny passages between the minute crystals through which the liquid rises.

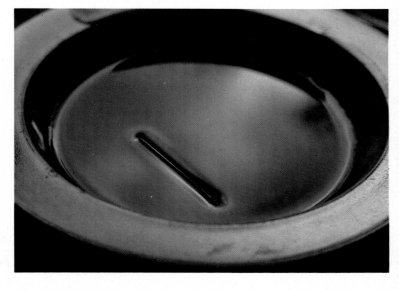

Challenge your friends to float a needle on water. It is quite easy so long as you remember that water has a 'skin' which must not be pierced. The 'skin' is a force called surface tension. Avoid piercing the surface by first placing the needle on a paper tissue and floating it gently on the water. The paper will become sodden and sink, leaving the needle on the surface.

Look and Listen

YOU CAN learn a lot about science even from a glass of water. Hold it up to eye level and you can see that the water climbs a little way up the sides of the glass. We call this a meniscus. It is the result of surface tension – forces exerted by the molecules in the surface layer (see page 33).

Look in the top of the glass and you will notice that the water appears to be much shallower than it really is. You notice the same effect in a swimming pool. Drop a spoon in the glass and look at it from the side at eye level. The handle of the spoon appears to be broken at the surface. Now turn the glass round until the spoon faces towards you, and you will notice that the part of the spoon beneath the surface is magnified. Raise the glass slightly and look at the underside of the surface; it has become a mirror.

Breaking and Speeding

The shallow bottom, the broken handle and the magnified image are effects caused by the way light behaves when it passes from one substance, or medium, to another. At the point where it passes between one medium and another, a ray of light bends, or is refracted. Because light rays from the bottom of the glass are refracted as they pass from water to air, they appear to come from a higher point. The same effect enables a wary fish in the water to see an angler on the bank, who thinks he is out of sight. So if you are after a fish, keep well back otherwise he will spot you.

When straws stand in a glass of water, they appear to be broken at the surface (right). This happens because light rays bend as they pass from one transparent substance to another. This is called refraction.

Lenses are curved pieces of glass, which bend light rays in predictable ways. They can make objects appear larger, smaller and upside down. The two most common kinds of lenses are the convex and the concave (below). The convex lens (bottom) brings together, or converges, light rays. The concave lens spreads out, or diverges, light rays.

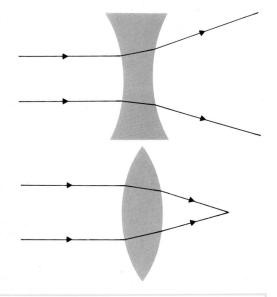

Refraction takes place because light travels at different speeds in different media. In air, it travels at some 300,000 kilometres per second. Water slows it down to about 225,000 km/sec; ordinary glass to about 200,000 km/sec and diamond, to about 124,000 km/sec. The amount light slows down as it passes from air to another substance is a measure of its refractive index. Diamond has a very high refractive index, which accounts for its sparkle and brilliance when cut.

Magnification

The magnification you can see in the glass comes about because the glass is curved. When light is refracted at curved surfaces, a magnified image can be produced. The water in the curved glass is acting like a convex lens (one which is wider in the middle than at the edges). A simple magnifying glass is a double convex lens, having curved surfaces on both sides. You can form different kinds of image with such a lens, depending on where you hold it in relation to the object you are viewing.

When you use the lens as a burning glass, you are bringing the sun's rays

---

MAKE A RAINBOW

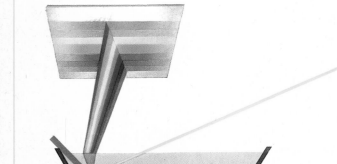

On a sunny day, fill a bowl with water and rest a flat mirror against the side. Draw the curtains of the room so that only a thin shaft of sunlight falls on the mirror. By adjusting the angle of the mirror you will be able to project a rainbow, or spectrum, on to a card or wall nearby. The 'wedge' of water between the mirror and the surface acts like a prism, and splits the incoming sunlight into its component colours.

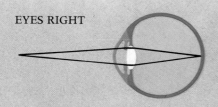
EYES RIGHT

Our eyes contain a lens which focuses light rays on to a screen, called the retina, at the back of the eyeball. Muscles in the eye can change the shape of the lens. They do this to bring light rays from different distances into focus on the retina.

Many people have poor eyesight because the lenses in their eyes are defective or their eyeballs are oddly shaped. As a result, light rays are not brought into focus on the retina. These people can correct their sight by wearing glass lenses, or spectacles, in front of their eyes.

When a person is short-sighted, he cannot focus on distant objects. His eyeballs are too long. Distant images come into focus in front of the retina. He can correct his sight by wearing spectacles with diverging, or concave, lenses.

When a person is long-sighted, he cannot focus on nearby objects. His eyeballs are too short, and nearby images are focused behind the retina. He can correct his sight by wearing spectacles with converging, or convex, lenses.

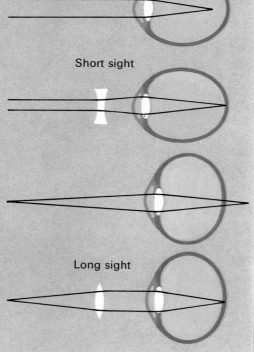

Short sight

Long sight

The Eye and the Camera
The lens in the eye is a convex lens, which can change its shape to bring light rays to a focus on the retina, a kind of screen at the back of the eye. A camera works in much the same way as an eye. It has a convex lens system which focuses an image on to a piece of film (like the retina). It has an opening over the lens which can open or close to regulate the light entering, just like the iris in your eye. Its shutter acts like the eyelid.

Like cameras and other man-made optical systems the eye can suffer from defects. They can often be corrected by spectacles (see panel left). The eye is also easily fooled (see page 36).

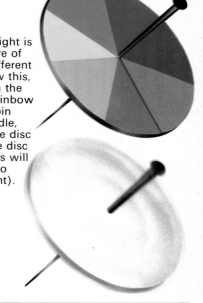

Ordinary white light is actually a mixture of light of many different colours. To show this, paint a disc with the colours of the rainbow (right). Stick a pin through the middle, and then spin the disc like a top. As the disc spins, the colours will merge together to make white (right).

to a point (the focus of the lens), where you can see a tiny image of the sun. The sun's heat as well as its light is concentrated at the focus, which is why that spot can burn. The sun's image is a real one; you can not only see it but could record it on film. When you use the convex lens as a magnifying glass, the image found is unreal, or virtual. Though you can see it with your eyes, you cannot record it on film.

A person with astigmatism cannot see anything plainly. Light rays are brought into focus both in front of and behind the retina. An odd-shaped lens is needed to correct this defect.

The Colours of Light
Another effect you often notice with a magnifying glass is that, near the edges, the image becomes blurred and is surrounded by a band, or spectrum, of rainbow colours. This occurs because light is not 'white' but composed of many different colours – indigo, violet, blue, green, yellow, orange and red – which add up to make white light. The colours are light of different wavelengths. Each colour travels at a slightly different speed, and is thus refracted through a slightly different angle. This has the effect of separating the colours, forming a spectrum. A prism of glass produces a good spectrum; so does a raindrop (see page 12).

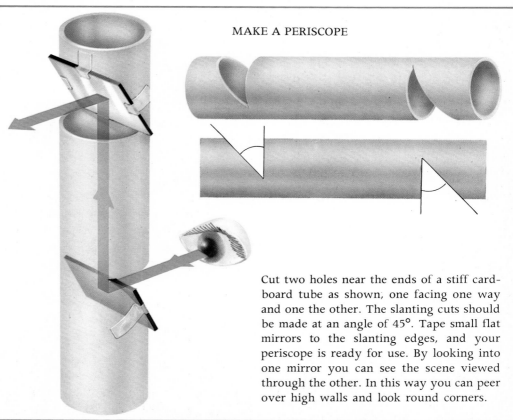

MAKE A PERISCOPE

Cut two holes near the ends of a stiff cardboard tube as shown, one facing one way and one the other. The slanting cuts should be made at an angle of 45°. Tape small flat mirrors to the slanting edges, and your periscope is ready for use. By looking into one mirror you can see the scene viewed through the other. In this way you can peer over high walls and look round corners.

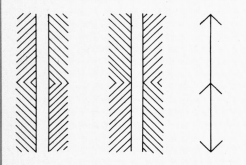
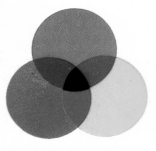

THE PRIMARY COLOURS

Everyone knows that green paint can be made by mixing equal quantities of blue and yellow paint together. If you wanted to, you could make paint of any colour, except white, by mixing together different amounts of blue, yellow and red. They are called the primary colours.

Any coloured light can be produced by mixing together different amounts of blue, green and red. These are the primary light colours. When all three are mixed together, white light is produced.

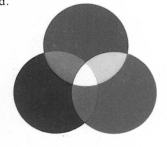

On Reflection

Glass and water are unusual because they allow through most of the light that falls on them. In other words, they are transparent. Most substances, however, do not let light pass through – they are opaque. All the light that falls on them is absorbed or reflected. The shiny substances we call mirrors reflect almost all the light falling on them. Ordinary mirrors consist of a flat sheet of glass with a very thin silvery coating on the back.

Like refraction, reflection deflects the path of light rays, and this property is made use of in many optical instruments. Flat mirrors are used to stagger the light path in a periscope, a simple instrument to make and fun to use (see panel, page 35). Curved mirrors are also widely used; like lenses, they can collect and focus light rays and often form a magnified image. Reflecting telescopes use concave, or saucer-shaped, mirrors to collect light, so do many vanity mirrors. But car wing-mirrors are often convex. They give the driver a wider field of view than a flat mirror, but a smaller image.

What is Colour?

Other opaque substances absorb as well as reflect light. They absorb light of some colours and reflect light of others. This determines the colour we see. A red object, for example, reflects red light but absorbs light of other colours. Colours have been 'subtracted' from white light by the object. Subtraction of colour also decides which colour results when paints are mixed. But when coloured lights are mixed, the result depends on the way the light wavelengths add together.

Sounds Interesting

Light travels in waves, which is why we speak of light wavelengths. Sound also travels in waves. They are both kinds of vibrations. Touch a bell that is ringing and you will feel the vibrations. Or strike a tuning fork and touch the surface of water with it, and you will see their effect.

Light is a vibration which can travel through empty space, as sunlight does. But sound is a vibration that needs a medium to travel in. A favourite school experiment shows this. Put an old fashioned alarm clock under a bell jar, and when it rings pump out the air. As the air disappears, so does the sound, though you can still see the striker hitting the bell.

A vibrating object sets the air molecules in contact with it vibrating too. These air molecules move back and forth, passing on their movement to the molecules next to them, which in turn do the same. Eventually the vibrations pass to the air molecules in your ear, and cause your eardrum to vibrate. Messages then go to the brain which recognizes them as sounds.

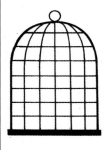
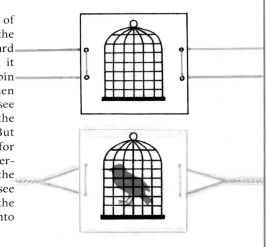
The Speed of Sound

Sound travels very much slower than light. When you look at someone hammering a long way off, you see the hammer strike before you hear the noise. You also see a lightning flash before you hear the thunder that accompanies it. You can easily work out how far away lightning is. It takes sound about three seconds to travel through a kilometre of air. So if you count the number of seconds between a lightning flash and thunder, then divide by three, you will know how far away the lightning is, in kilometres. Sound travels better through liquids and solids than it does through air and other gases. In liquids and solids the molecules are much closer together than they are in a gas. This means that they do not have to move so far to 'nudge' the next molecules. As a result, the vibrations, or sounds, travel more quickly. Sound travels four times faster in water than in air, and 15 times faster in steel.

Louder and Louder
The denser a substance is, the less it absorbs from vibrations passing through it, and the louder will be the resultant sound. Tap on a table top with your finger and listen. Now press your ear to the table and tap again. The sound is very much louder. Not only have the vibrations passed through it more efficiently, but they have been channelled along a restricted path – the table top – instead of spreading in all directions in the air.

Demonstrate this another way with a spoon hung on a piece of string. Holding it away from you, strike the

air in the carton vibrates as you speak into it and sets the base of the carton vibrating. The string carries these vibrations to the base of the other carton. This vibrates the air inside, which carries sound to the receiver's ear.

Sound Mirrors
Sound can be reflected from objects just as light can. You can have great fun experimenting with umbrellas, which act like curved sound mirrors to concentrate the sound. Echoes are sound waves that have been reflected from distant walls or cliffs. If you find a spot in the mountains where you can shout and get a clear echo, you can easily work out how far away the reflecting face is. For each two second delay, the cliff is three kilometres away. (Why 2 secs per 3 km?)

Strike a Note of Sympathy
Sometimes, an object making one sound sets up a similar sound in another object nearby. This is called resonance and you can demonstrate it in a very melodious way. Put a little water into two wine glasses so that they each

give you a similar note when struck. Place them a few centimetres apart. Moisten your finger and slowly rub the rim of one glass. It will give out a beautiful sound, rather like a harmonica. Soon the second glass will start singing, even though you are not touching it. The vibrations from the first glass are causing it to vibrate in sympathy, or in resonance. Notice what happens to the surface of the water in each glass. You can also demonstrate resonance with two violins laid side by side. If you pluck the A string of one, the A string of the other will start to sound too.

High or Low
The pitch (highness or lowness) of notes produced by a stringed instrument depends on the length and tautness of the strings. A long, loose string vibrates slowly (at a low frequency) and therefore gives a low note. When the string is made shorter and tighter it vibrates more quickly (at a higher frequency) and produces a higher note. You can demonstrate these principles with elastic bands. When you have

When a column of air vibrates, it gives out a musical note. As its length changes, so does the note. Prove it with this simple musical instrument (right). Blow across the open top, and move the piston (knitting needle and cork) up and down. The note changes as the piston rises and falls.

A recorder player (left) closes different holes to change the length of the vibrating air column. In this way she produces different notes.

You can make a simple guitar from a cardboard shoebox (right) and some elastic bands. Cut a hole in the lid of the box and tack lengths of band of varying thickness to it. Fit a wedge of wood beneath the bands as shown. The bands will give out different notes when they are plucked.

By rubbing the rim of a partly filled wine glass with a wet finger (below), you can produce beautiful sounds. You can make a glass harmonica using several glasses filled to different levels.

Sound travels better through string than it does through air. You can make a telephone (left) using string to carry the sound. The mouthpiece and earpiece can be cans or yoghurt cartons

spoon. You will hear a bell-like note. Press the string against your ear, and the bell sound will grow louder as it travels up the string. By adding different forks, spoons and other metal objects to your string, you can make a tuneful carillon, or peal of bells.

A String Telephone
Using string to carry the sound, make yourself a telephone. Simply attach a yoghurt or cream carton to each end of a length of string. The cartons act both as mouthpiece and earpiece. The

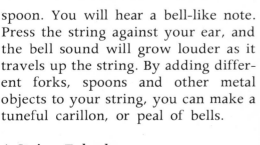

done so, try making a zither, with your bands 'tuned' to different pitches.

Wind instruments such as the recorder and flute produce their music by vibrating a tube, or column, of air. By 'fingering' their instruments, players change the length of the air column inside. When the length changes, so does the rate of vibration, or note produced. You can easily demonstrate this. Fill up a row of wine bottles to different levels and then blow across the top of them. They will produce different notes.

Stay at Home

IF YOU THINK about it, your home is a kind of scientific laboratory in which every member of your family is a scientist. For, in a home, every day, a large number of quite complicated scientific experiments are carried out and each day the marvels of technology are put to the test. For instance, every time you wash up you are performing a tried and tested experiment, proving yet again that the molecules in the detergent attach themselves to greasy particles, lift them and dissolve them in water. Still in the kitchen – where most of home chemical experiments take place – you can easily demonstrate the 'three states of matter'. Take water (in its liquid state from the tap – and what is the principle behind a tap?); put the water in your fridge's ice compartment and you have water in its solid state; by boiling water you produce water gas which quickly turns into steam to condense on the walls as liquid water again.

There are dozens of everyday 'household' experiments you can find out about. What happens when you burn the toast; why does cream always rise to the top in the milk bottle; what makes a cake rise, and so on?

Simple Machines

Every day in your home you use all the six basic forms of simple machines. Every time you lift something you are using a *lever* (your arm). When you use nutcrackers or scissors you are also using levers. Chisels and axes are forms of *wedges*. A *pulley* is used to raise the week's washing on the line. Your garden wheelbarrow has a *wheel* and axle. The principles of these simple machines are made use of in different combinations in far more complicated machines – in food mixers, washing machines and vacuum cleaners (and why the name vacuum cleaner?).

Many of our household gadgets – our irons, toasters, shavers, fridges and so on – all work by electricity. Today it would be difficult to imagine a home without electricity. We make electricity work for us in hundreds

CHEMICALS IN THE HOME

We use an enormous variety of chemicals in our everyday lives. We eat them, cook with them, wash with them, and rely on them to cure our aches and pains.

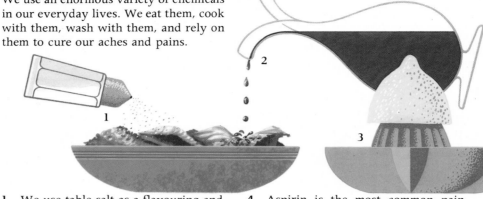

1   We use table salt as a flavouring and preserving agent. Its chemical name is sodium chloride. It is one of many chemicals called salts.
2   Vinegar contains acetic acid. Its sharp flavour makes salads more appetizing and it helps preserve foods.
3   Lemon juice is citric acid.

4   Aspirin is the most common pain-killer that we use as medicine. It is an acid called acetyl salicylic acid. When you have an upset stomach you need, not an acid, but an antacid. This contains an alkali, which fights the acidity.
5   Some fabrics shrink or lose their colour in soap and water, so they must

SIMPLE MACHINES

A machine is something that helps us do work. Many modern machines are very complicated, but they are in fact combinations of much simpler machines.

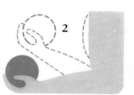
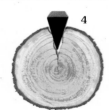

A crowbar (1) is a simple form of lever which enables you to move a heavy load. Your arm (2) is also a lever. So is the wheelbarrow (3). Its wheel and axle are also a simple machine. The inclined plane, or slope, is so simple that it hardly seems to be a machine, but it is a means of doing something more easily.

Can you tip up a bucket of water without spilling it? It is easy when you know how. Swing the bucket rapidly round in a circle over your head. Then the water will be held in the bucket by centrifugal force. This is a force that acts away from the centre on something moving in a circle.

38

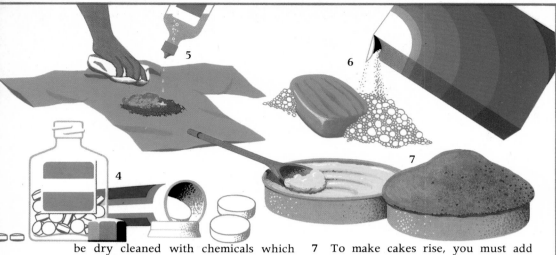

of ways – to light lamps, make the television and telephone work, to heat water and make the record player go round. So what is this amazing source of energy; how is it made? To find out we should first examine the intriguing property of magnetism.

Pins and Needles

If one of your hobbies is collecting rocks and minerals, you may have a specimen of magnetite (lodestone). With this mineral you can pick up pins, needles, paper clips, and indeed anything made of iron and steel, for it is a natural magnet. If you have no magnetite look in your mother's sewing box. She might have a proper magnet to pick up pins with.

Proper magnets are cheaper and more powerful than magnetite, so they

be dry cleaned with chemicals which dissolve grease and stains and evaporate quickly.

6 Soaps are made from strong alkalis called caustic soda and caustic potash. Detergents are more powerful cleansing agents. They are made from chemicals obtained from petroleum, or crude oil.

7 To make cakes rise, you must add baking powder to the cake mixture (unless it is already in the flour). Baking powder contains a chemical called bicarbonate of soda. When this is heated, it gives off carbon dioxide gas. As the gas tries to escape, it makes the mixture rise, and you get a light cake.

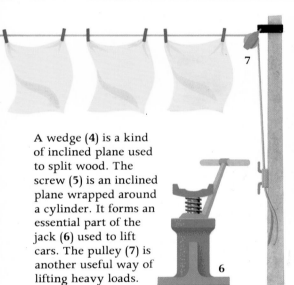

A wedge (4) is a kind of inclined plane used to split wood. The screw (5) is an inclined plane wrapped around a cylinder. It forms an essential part of the jack (6) used to lift cars. The pulley (7) is another useful way of lifting heavy loads.

The garden sprinkler works on the same principle as the rocket, the principle of reaction. As water streams backwards out of the nozzles, there is equal force forwards, which makes the sprinkler spin round.

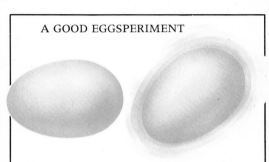

A GOOD EGGSPERIMENT

Take two eggs, and boil one. How can you tell which one is boiled? Spin them, and then stop them suddenly. One remains still afterwards, but the other starts to spin again. The one that remains still is the boiled one. The raw egg starts to spin again because it has liquid inside, which is still moving.

are better for experiments. A simple bar magnet is best. Suspend your magnet by a thread, so that it can swing freely, and you will notice that it always comes to rest in the same position. One end of the magnet will always point south and the other will always point north. Label one end of your magnet N (north pointing) and the other end S (south pointing).

Raid your mother's sewing box again for a steel knitting needle, and stroke it several times in the same direction with a magnet (see page 40). Then suspend the needle by a thread. It too will always come to rest in the same position. You have turned it into a magnet.

It is easy to make a compass using magnetized needles. You can mount them on a card, or you can stick them through a cork floating on a saucer of water.

ROLL UP! ROLL UP!

100 mm

25 mm

200 mm

25 mm

180 mm

6 mm

This is a fascinating trick in which an object appears to defy gravity. Make the double cone shown from stiff paper or a large candle. Cut the sloping track from stiff cardboard or plywood. If you keep to the dimensions shown, the trick will work. Place the track in a V shape with the lower ends close together. Put the cone at the bottom and, if all goes well, the cone will proceed to roll upwards!

What's the Attraction?

By bringing different ends, or poles, of two magnets together, you can discover the basic laws of magnetism. Bring a N pole close to a S, and they attract one another. But bring a N pole close to another N, or a S pole up to another S and you can feel a force pushing them apart. Remember, unlike magnetic poles attract, like poles repel.

When you bring two poles together you can feel the force attracting them or pushing them apart. Think of the

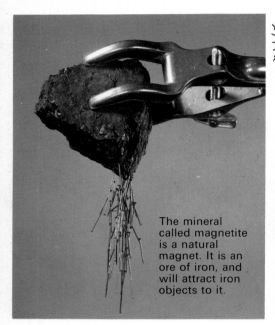

The mineral called magnetite is a natural magnet. It is an ore of iron, and will attract iron objects to it.

magnets as being surrounded by currents of water flowing out of the north pole and into the south pole. When unlike poles are close together the currents combine and strengthen each other (attract). When like poles are close together, the currents battle against each other and repel.

You can show the path of the so-called magnetic currents with iron filings. You can either sprinkle the filings directly on to the magnet (see pictures), or you can put a card over the magnet and sprinkle the filings on top. Tap the card gently and gradually the filings will line themselves up into loops. We call these loops lines of force, and the region where the magnetic force acts, the magnetic field.

You can plot lines of force in another way. Put a card over your magnet as before and place a compass in various positions around it and at different distances from it. In each position draw on the card the direction in which the compass needle is pointing. Is the pattern you get the same as that made by the iron filings?

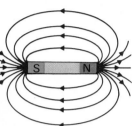

The shape of the magnetic field of force around a magnet can be shown with the help of iron filings. When they are sprinkled around a magnet, they form into loops between the ends, or poles, of the magnet.

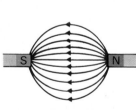

When the pole of one magnet is brought near the pole of another, the magnetic fields affect one another. When one is a north pole and the other a south pole, lines of force link the two magnets. The magnets are drawn together.

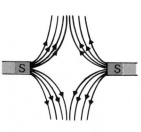

When, however, a north pole is brought near another north pole, the magnetic lines of force loop away from each other. The same thing happens when two south poles are brought together. The magnets push each other away.

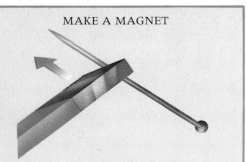

MAKE A MAGNET

Once you have one magnet, you can easily make others – from steel knitting needles for example. All you do is hold the needle in one hand and stroke it a number of times with one end of your magnet, always in the same direction. Lift the magnet high in the air after each stroke. If you use the north pole of the magnet to stroke the needle, the end of the needle farthest away from you will be a south pole.

. . . AND A COMPASS

With magnetized needles you can make a compass. Fold a small piece of card and push the needles through, making sure that the north poles of the needles are on the same side. Balance the card on an upturned drawing pin set in plasticine to keep it steady. Mark the compass points on the baseboard and your compass is ready to use. When you let the card go, it will swing round so that the north poles of the needles point north.

The World Magnet

When your compass is within the magnet's force field, the needle points steadily in a certain direction. When you bring another magnet near it, the needle swings and points steadily in a different direction. When you take them both away, the needle swings and points in yet another direction just as steadily as before. So it must still be in the grip of a magnet. This magnet is the earth itself.

The earth behaves as if it has a gigantic bar magnet buried inside it, with one end roughly at the north pole and the other roughly at the south pole. The lines of force between the two run very nearly north–south. That is why a compass needle always aligns itself in that direction, if no greater force is acting on it. The compass direction is not quite identical to true north and south, and when you are map-reading with a compass, you have to allow for this.

The Magnet Puzzle

If you have observed your iron filings

experiments closely, you will be able to work out how to do the following puzzle. There are two identical steel knitting needles, one is magnetized, the other is not. How can you find which one is magnetized? You are not allowed to suspend them on threads, float them on corks, or touch other metals with them.

This is quite tricky, because if you touch the end of one needle with another, you cannot tell which is doing the attracting and which is being attracted. The secret lies in touching the middle of one with the tip of the other. If you are holding the magnet, you will pick up the other needle. If you are holding the unmagnetized needle, you will not pick up the other.

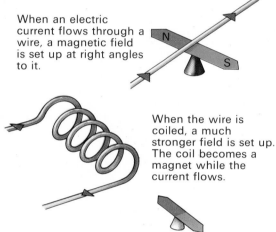

When an electric current flows through a wire, a magnetic field is set up at right angles to it.

When the wire is coiled, a much stronger field is set up. The coil becomes a magnet while the current flows.

How to Kill a Magnet
In the iron filings experiment, the filings cluster round the ends of the magnet not the middle, which appears to be unmagnetized. But is it? Cut a magnetized needle in two with wire cutters (be careful!). Do you get a one-ended magnet? Can you get rid of the magnetism by cutting off both ends of the needle? You find in each case that you end up, not with parts of the original magnet but with new complete magnets. If you want to get rid of a needle's magnetism, heat it in a flame until it is red hot, or hammer it for a while.

Before killing your magnet, see if it attracts metals other than iron or steel. What do you find?

Electrical Magnetism
Magnets are not the only things that produce a magnetic field. A field is also produced when an electric current passes through a wire. The wire does not have to be made of iron either. Place a single copper wire over the needle of your compass and then

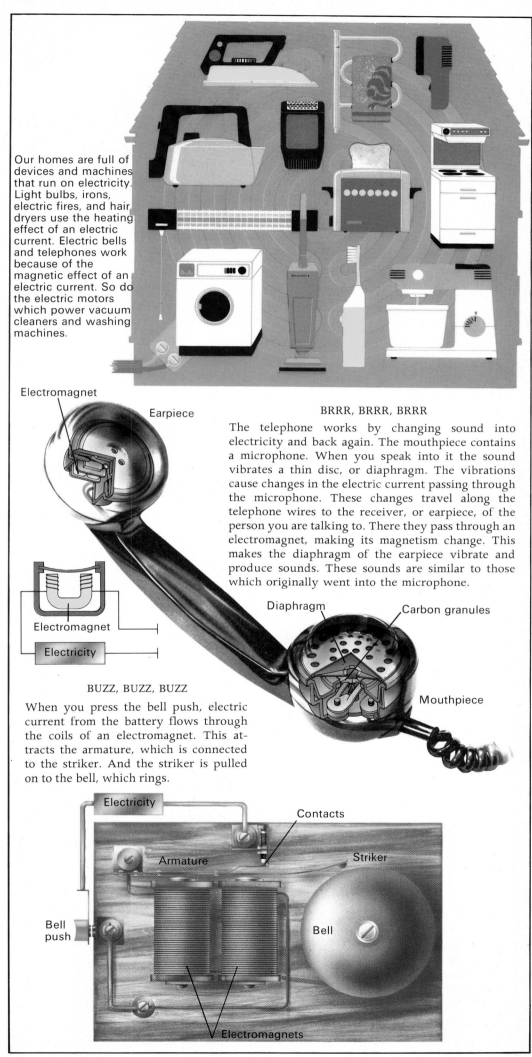

Our homes are full of devices and machines that run on electricity. Light bulbs, irons, electric fires, and hair dryers use the heating effect of an electric current. Electric bells and telephones work because of the magnetic effect of an electric current. So do the electric motors which power vacuum cleaners and washing machines.

Electromagnet

Earpiece

BRRR, BRRR, BRRR
The telephone works by changing sound into electricity and back again. The mouthpiece contains a microphone. When you speak into it the sound vibrates a thin disc, or diaphragm. The vibrations cause changes in the electric current passing through the microphone. These changes travel along the telephone wires to the receiver, or earpiece, of the person you are talking to. There they pass through an electromagnet, making its magnetism change. This makes the diaphragm of the earpiece vibrate and produce sounds. These sounds are similar to those which originally went into the microphone.

Electromagnet

Electricity

Diaphragm

Carbon granules

Mouthpiece

BUZZ, BUZZ, BUZZ
When you press the bell push, electric current from the battery flows through the coils of an electromagnet. This attracts the armature, which is connected to the striker. And the striker is pulled on to the bell, which rings.

Electricity

Contacts

Armature

Striker

Bell push

Bell

Electromagnets

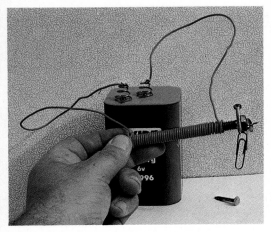

You can make a simple electromagnet by winding wire around an iron bolt. When you connect the ends of the wire to a battery, the bolt becomes a strong magnet. It loses its magnetism when the battery is disconnected.

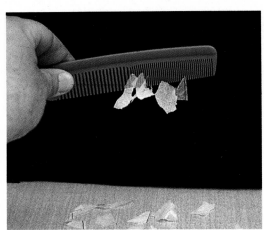

When you comb your hair, both the comb and your hair become charged with electricity. On a dry day you can sometimes hear the electricity crackling through your hair. Your electrified comb can attract bits of paper to it just as a magnet attracts bits of iron.

touch the terminals of a torch battery with the ends of the wire. When the current flows, the needle swings to one side. It returns to its original position when you disconnect the battery. What happens when you reverse the battery terminals? The science that deals with the connexion between magnetism and electricity is called electromagnetism.

Make a Solenoid

You can increase the magnetic 'power' of a wire carrying electricity by winding it into coils. Wind a length of insulated copper wire (you can buy it from electrical shops) around a cardboard tube (several turns) and connect the ends to a battery. Place a card over the coil and sprinkle some iron filings on top. Tap the card and see the pattern the filings make. It should be similar to the pattern around your bar magnet, for a coil carrying a current has the same effect as a bar magnet. It is called a solenoid.

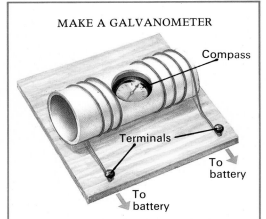

MAKE A GALVANOMETER

Compass

Terminals

To battery

To battery

You can make a galvanometer (an instrument to detect electric current) very simply. Cut a window out of a cardboard tube. Then wind many turns of insulated copper wire around the tube, to form two coils on either side of the window. Stick the tube to a baseboard and fix the ends of the wire to two eye-screw terminals. Place a small compass beneath the window, inside the tube. Your galvanometer is now ready for use. When electric current flows through the coil, the compass needle will be deflected.

See if your solenoid will pick up tin-tacks or paper clips. If it will not, try a stronger battery or connect several batteries together to produce a more powerful current. And wind the coil more. Then see if the solenoid has a north and south pole like a bar magnet. Test this with your bar magnets. How does changing the direction in which the current is flowing affect the magnetism of your coil?

Increase Your Attraction

You will notice that your solenoid is only magnetic while the electric current flows. If you place a thick iron bolt inside it, the magnetism is much increased. The iron concentrates the magnetic line of force. You now have made a simple electromagnet and will be able to attract larger iron objects.

You can convert a solenoid into a sensitive current detector, called a galvanometer (see panel). You will need a galvanometer in the next experiment.

Off and On

Wind many turns of insulated copper wire around each end of a long iron bolt. Connect the ends of one coil through a simple switch to a battery, and the ends of the other coil to your galvanometer. With the switch open, the galvanometer needle remains steady. Keep looking at the needle and close the switch. Notice that the needle kicks. Switch off and the needle kicks again, but in the opposite direction.

By switching the current in the first coil on and off you have set up, or induced, a wave of electricity in the second coil, even though they are not connected. This principle is known as electromagnetic induction. Electricity transformers, which change the voltage of mains electricity between power stations and user, work by electromagnetic induction.

ELECTRICITY WITH A KICK

You can use the simple apparatus pictured below to show the principle on which the electric motor works. Position the wire loop between the poles of a horseshoe magnet, and make sure that the loop can swing freely in its supports. Make a circuit by connecting the supports through a simple switch to a battery. Press the switch and you will see the loop give a sharp kick.

Turn the magnet over and try again. The loop kicks, but in the opposite direction. Reverse the battery terminals and repeat.

The loop kicks in the original direction once more, for you have reversed both the direction of the magnetic field and the electric current.

Remove the magnet and repeat the experiment. Nothing happens, you can now state your conclusions. To obtain a motor effect – a kick – you need both a magnetic field and an electric current. The direction of movement depends on the direction of the field and the current. A practical motor has many loops, or coils, of wire and an iron core to intensify the magnetic field.

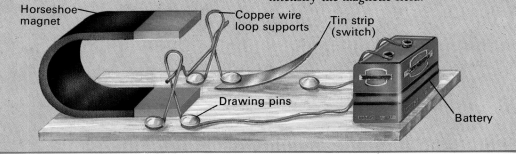

Horseshoe magnet

Copper wire loop supports

Tin strip (switch)

Drawing pins

Battery

Be Dynamic

Wind another coil around a cardboard tube and connect the ends to the galvanometer. With your eyes on the galvanometer needle, thrust a bar magnet into the middle of the coil. The needle will kick while the magnet is moving. Keep the magnet still, and the needle will remain steady. Withdraw the magnet from the coil, and the needle will kick again, but in the opposite direction.

Think what is happening. The kick of the needle shows that you have set up an electric current in the coil by moving a magnet nearby. Now keep the magnet still and move the coil. The needle will kick again, and you will have demonstrated the dynamo effect, which is the principle behind all electricity generators. When a wire moves in a magnetic field, an electric current is set up in it.

You can also set up a simple experiment to show the reverse of the dynamo effect (see page 42). When a wire is carrying an electric current in a magnetic field, it moves. This is the principle behind the electric motor.

Chemical Electricity

The mains electricity we use in our homes is produced by generators using the electromagnetic effect. Torch batteries produce electricity by chemical action. Place two different metals, say copper and zinc, in a salt solution, and connect them to the ends of your galvanometer. The kick of the needle, shows that electricity is flowing from the copper rod to the zinc.

Repeat the same experiment using rods (electrodes) of different metals in different chemical solutions (electrolytes). Carbon, which is not a metal, also makes a good electrode. You can get carbon rods from spent torch batteries. The battery casing is zinc, which also makes good electrodes. You can make a wet version of the 'dry' torch battery by putting the carbon and zinc electrodes into a solution of ammonium chloride, which is also the active chemical in dry batteries. Try lighting a torch bulb from your battery.

Just as chemical action can produce electricity, so electricity can produce chemical action. Remember the experiment on page 32 where electricity was used to split water into its constituents – hydrogen and oxygen. We call the splitting up of a substance by electricity, electrolysis.

An Electric Blanket

Electricity is used to coat or plate objects with metal: this is called electroplating. You can give unattractive metals like iron a shiny, rust-proof coating of silver or copper (see panel). Try making simple badges from tin, and plating them with copper. Afterwards, give them a coat of clear lacquer to prevent them tarnishing.

Static Electricity

The kind of electricity you have been using is called current electricity, because it flows. There is another type of electricity which does not flow, called static electricity. Using static electricity you can make a comb into a 'magnet' simply by combing your hair. Rubbing the comb against your hair gives it an electric charge and enables it to pick up pieces of paper.

You can give many things an electric charge in a similar way – silk, ebony, glass, nylon, rubber, bakelite and other plastics. You can charge these materials because they are insulators: they do not conduct electricity. If they did, the electricity would just leak away. It is best to experiment with static electricity on a dry day. When there is moisture in the air, the static electricity leaks away faster.

On a dry day, when your hair is also very dry, combing may produce a crackling noise. This is because you are generating high-voltage electricity! On such a day comb your hair vigorously and hold your comb a few millimetres from a tap. If you are lucky, you may see a spark jump between your comb and the tap. A gigantic spark caused by static electricity is produced in thunderclouds – we call it lightning.

Rub a balloon briskly against your clothes to charge it with electricity. Then let it cling 'magically' to the ceiling.

MAKE A COPPER MEDALLION

You can use the chemical effect of an electric current to give cheap metals an attractive coating. Cut out a medallion from a piece of tin or an oil can. Clean both sides with emery paper and attach a copper wire to it. Attach a piece of copper (copper tubing for example) to another wire. Fix the free ends of the wires to a battery, the copper to the positive (+) terminal and the tin to the negative (−). Now dip the copper and tin pieces into a solution of copper sulphate. Leave this circuit set up for a while, and you will find that the tin gradually becomes coated with a layer of copper. When the layer is even all over, remove your shiny medallion, wash it, and coat it with a clear lacquer to preserve its colour.

Using the same apparatus, amaze your friends and relations by turning their 'silver' coins into 'copper' ones!

BOOKS TO READ

There are a great many interesting and fascinating books available to give the budding scientist greater understanding of the subjects we have introduced in *Science All Around*. The following list gives just a few of the many titles that are currently in print which you should find in most bookshops and libraries.

In addition to these books on individual topics there are several useful and up-to-date science encyclopedias available, including Sampson Low's *Great World of Science* and Purnell's *Concise Encyclopedia of Science*.

The Sky by Day
Flash, Crash, Rumble and Roll, by F. M. Branley (A & C Black)
About Our Weather, by G. H. Gibson (Muller)
Interpreting the Weather – A Practical Guide, by I. Holford (David & Charles)
First Look at the Weather, by Robin Kerrod (Watts)
Observer's Book of the Weather, by R. M. Lester (Warne)
Instant Weather Forecasting, by A. Watts (Adlard Coles)

The Sky by Night
Astronomy for the Amateur, John Gribbin (Macmillan)
Colour Guide to Stars and Planets, by Robin Kerrod (Ward Lock)
Astronomy in Colour, P. Lancaster Brown (Blandford)
Observer's Book of Astronomy, by Patrick Moore (Warne)
Guide to the Moon, by Patrick Moore (Lutterworth)
Exploring the Planets, by Iain Nicholson (Hamlyn)

Norton's Star Atlas, by A. P. Norton (Gall & Inglis)
This invaluable reference handbook has charts showing 9000 stars, clusters and nebulae, and lists detailing some of the most interesting objects to look at.

Uphill and Down Dale
Exploring Crystals, by J. Berry (Collier)
Field Guide to Rocks and Minerals, by J. Bauer (Octopus)
Observer's Book of Rocks and Minerals, by Rhona Black (Warne)
Fun with Geology, by W. C. Cartner (Kaye and Ward)
Pebbles on the Beach, by C. Ellis (Faber)
Finding Fossils, by Roger Hamilton and Allan Insole (Kestrel)
Focus on Earth, by A. & D. Lucas (Methuen)
Our Planet Earth, by Keith Lye (Ward Lock)
Fossils in Colour, by J. F. Kirkaldy (Blandford)
Volcanoes, by W. Kirst (Hart-Davis)
Introduction to the Mineral Kingdom, R. M. Pearl (Blandford)
Rocks, Minerals and Gemstones, by I. O. Evans (Hamlyn)
The Earth Tells Its Story, by W. E. Swinton (Bodley Head)
In addition the Geological Museum in London produces some excellent booklets, for example on *The Earth* and *Volcanoes*. When you are in London, visit the Geological Museum in South Kensington. You will not only see the wonders of the mineral kingdom but also displays showing how geological processes take place. Round the corner from the Museum is the Natural History Museum, which exhibits fine fossils of creatures that have long passed from the face of the Earth. The museum leads directly into the Science Museum itself.

Look and Listen
Your Book of Light, by T. Gunston (Faber)
First Book of Light, G. Harrison (Watts)
Fun with Photography, T. Hart and J. Harley (Kaye and Ward)
Cameras Work Like This, by M. Kidd (Phoenix)
Light, Mirrors and Lenses, by F. Newing and R. Bowood (Ladybird)
Pocket Money Photography, by Chris Wright (Severn House)
First Book of Sound, by David Knight (Watts)
Sound and Hearing (Time-Life)
Shake, Rattle and Bang, by G. Wolde (A & C Black)

Stay at Home
Burke Book of Modern Chemical Wonders (Burke)
Fun with Chemistry, by I & M Freeman (Kaye and Ward)
Chemistry Experiments, by A. Kemper (Burke)
Chemistry by Experiment, P. Roberson (Hart-Davis)
Magnets, by I. and R. Adler (Dobson)
Junior Science Book of Magnets, by R. V. Feravolo (Muller)
First Book of Electricity, S. and B. Epstein (Watts)
Fun with Electricity, by C. Siddons (Kaye and Ward)
Magnets, Bulbs and Batteries, by F. Newing and R. Bowood (Ladybird)
Heat and Temperature, by J. Bendick (Watts)
Taking the Temperature, by David Fishlock (Deutsch)
Young Scientists Book of Cold/Heat, by M. Kentzer (Collins)

ONE LAST TRICK

Balance a long cane on your fingers so that one end overhangs, as in the picture (left). Now bring your fingers slowly together. You might think that the cane would over-balance on the overhanging side, but you would be wrong.

The cane, in fact, remains in perfect balance throughout, and your fingers will end up together in the middle (right). The secret of the balancing act lies in friction. The friction between the cane and each finger is different, and this causes the cane to remain in balance as your fingers move.

Index

Numerals in *italics* indicate illustrations

ACKNOWLEDGEMENTS

The author would particularly like to thank Abigail Ride for appearing in many of the photographs he took for the book; Michael Chinery, for supplying additional photographs; and Barry Fox, for helpful suggestions on the text and illustrations.

PICTURE CREDITS

The pictures on the following pages were kindly supplied by the author: 9 bottom & right; 11 right; 15; 16 right; 19; 20 left; 23 bottom; 24; 25 left; 26 centre; 27 top left & centre; 29 top & inset; 38; 39; 42; 44.

Other pictures were supplied by the following: All Sport 8 top; Australian Pearl Company 26 & 27 Nos 2, 4, 6, 9, 10, 11, 12; California Institute of Technology 16 left, 20 right, 21 right; Michael Chinery 28 left, 30, 31 bottom right, 33, 37, 43; Dr Leo Connolly 21 top; Icelandic Tourist Office 23 top; Institute of Geological Sciences 26 & 27 Nos 1, 3, 5, 7, 8; Neil Lorrimer Endpapers, title pages, 8 right, 28 bottom right, 31 top, 32 top, 34, 40; Spectrum Colour Library 12; Starfoto 11 left; Zefa 10, 22, 25 right.

Artwork by The Tudor Art Agency